Policy Studies in Ageing
no 3

Triple jeopardy:

growing old in a

second homeland

Alison Norman

Centre for Policy on Ageing

First published 1985 by the
Centre for Policy on Ageing
Nuffield Lodge Studio
Regent's Park
London NW1 4RS

ISBN 0 904 139 42 5

Printed in Great Britain by
Henry Ling Ltd, The Dorset Press, Dorchester, Dorset, England

Contents

Foreword

The English language has many limitations, and one of them is that there are no simple words or single words which accurately describe people who came to the UK as adults and are now growing old. To call them 'elderly', as if their chronological age is their key characteristic is misleading, since few have yet reached extreme old age and many in their fifties and early sixties suffer the disabilities and disadvantages commonly associated with ageing. To call them 'immigrants' is technically correct, but the word has become unacceptable because it has been misused to describe members of ethnic minority groups and especially people of Asian and Afro-Caribbean descent who were born in the UK. Further, it is felt that to call people who have lived in this country for many years 'immigrants' implies that they will never be accepted as integral members of British society. 'Settler' is a preferred term, but this has echoes of the colonial era which some find disturbing. Both words are used in the text as seemed appropriate in the particular context, but it must be emphasised that they are used in their literal and correct meaning.

The phrase 'ethnic minority group' also has its drawbacks, since it, too, is often used to refer only to people of Afro-Caribbean or Asian descent, and it ignores the fact that in some wards of our 'inner' cities the 'ethnic minorities' are, in fact, the majority of the population. In this study 'ethnic minority group' refers to people of any race who see themselves as sharing a common culture which is distinct from that of the majority of the population as a whole. Such phrases and the use of 'umbrella' terms such as the 'Chinese community' or the 'Polish community' inevitably over-simplify the real situation and ignore the complexity and the richness of the many sub-groups which make up any particular culture. This is inevitable, but the study warns again and again that, in reviewing and planning local services, the composition of the particular population concerned demands careful and detailed enquiry.

Since the study covers the provision of services to members of ethnic minority groups of all kinds, the terms 'black' and 'white' have been avoided as far as possible except when quoting from other sources, but the report recognises that racial discrimination is a major and often dominant factor in hindering access to services and facilities, and that every effort must be made to combat racism in all its forms.

The study does not pretend to be based on any formal or systematic 'research'. After desk study and a pilot field enquiry (briefly described on p. 9), some forty clubs, day centres and sheltered housing initiatives run by members of the various ethnic minority groups for the benefit of their own elderly members were visited. The information thus obtained was used, not only to provide a basis for discussing the achievements and difficulties of these developments, but also as a means of reviewing barriers to use of other services. The visits were followed up by discussion with relevant members of local authorities, voluntary organisations, community relations councils and with other key informants. Shortage of time made it inevitable that ease of access and ready availability of contacts determined the places chosen for visits and the main focus has been on the London Boroughs of Brent, Haringey and Lambeth and the city of Birmingham, though projects in other parts of London and in Nottingham, Leicester, Coventry, Wolverhampton, Leeds and Bradford have also been included. It is regrettable that in the time available it was not possible to take in Manchester, Liverpool or Cardiff and the study is therefore lacking, not only in its coverage of developments in these cities but also its lack of reference to the British people of African, Caribbean, Asian and Chinese descent who belong to long-established ethnic minority communities in ports such as Bristol, Liverpool and Cardiff, and who are now old.

In spite of the limitations in its scope it is hoped that this study will prove to be a practical and positive contribution to the action which is urgently needed to make all our services, both statutory and voluntary, accessible to all elderly people who need them.

Acknowledgements

Grateful thanks are due to the Department of Health and Social Security which commissioned this study and to the officers of the Department for their encouragement and help while it was being prepared. Thanks are also due to the staff and members of the clubs, day centres, and sheltered housing developments which were visited in the course of the project for their generous welcome and their willingness to discuss their work and share their views. I am also most grateful to the officers of local authorities, staff of community relations councils and other key informants who contributed their knowledge and experience and offered detailed and most helpful comment when the report was in draft form.

Amongst my colleagues at CPA, I would particularly like to thank Jeanne Isaacs, who provided invaluable assistance in setting up appointments and processing data, and Nancy Klein who typed and retyped the drafts and final text.

Alison Norman
November 1984

1 The meaning of 'triple jeopardy'

'I, a stranger and afraid
In a world I never made'

Introduction

A E Housman's couplet poignantly reflects the feelings of thousands of refugees from political and racial persecution, 'displaced persons' made homeless by war, and people who came to Britain as much-needed workers. They have grown old in this country but still feel themselves to be strangers here, set apart from the indigenous 'ethnic majority', far from their former homelands, and even cut off from the younger generation of their own community who have grown up in Britain. Too often they are also living in conditions of loneliness, fear, sickness and privation in our inner cities. This, of course, is not the plight of all elderly settlers in this country and it is the plight of many indigenous elderly people who also feel themselves to be 'strangers and afraid' in a hostile world. Nevertheless, the acuteness of the isolation of those who by reason of language, culture, skin colour or religious belief find themselves unable to gain access to treatment, support and care does justify the title of this report. They are not merely in double jeopardy by reason of age and discrimination, as has often been stated, but in *triple* jeopardy, at risk because they are old, because of the physical conditions and hostility under which they have to live, *and* because services are not accessible to them. It is the purpose of this report to spell out how these risks can be reduced. It is addressed to the ethnic minority communities who can do, and are already doing, a great deal to support their own elderly members; to statutory health and social services; to grant-giving agencies; and to established voluntary organisations. But it is also addressed to the general public because, in the last resort, whatever efforts are made to improve the quality of service provision, it is the warmth and genuine friendliness of day-to-day contact between ordinary people which will enable these elders to feel they belong in their second homeland and to contribute their own wealth of experience to a truly multi-cultural society.

Awareness of the seriousness of the need has been with us for some time. Attention was drawn to it at a seminar organised by the Beth Johnson Foundation and the Commission for Racial Equality in 1979.[1] Almost every subsequent report in this field has carried some token reference to the growing population of elders in the ethnic minority groups who are at risk. But although much has been said, very little has been done to remedy the situation except by the ethnic minority groups themselves. One reason for this may be that those who are most committed to eliminating ethnic disadvantage often know little about services for the elderly, while those concerned for the elderly may not be in the forefront of the fight for non-discrimination. Another factor is that services for elderly people in general have developed over the years as a piecemeal response to demographic change, particular legislation, financial incentives and fashions in service provision. Until recently, very little has been done to get back to basics and think through what kinds of help are needed and how the needs can be most effectively and acceptably met. Indeed, one of the questions which the whole issue of care for older people with particular ethnic characteristics forces us to face is the appropriateness and efficiency of our services for *all* elderly people. They are still too often provided on the basis of inadequate one-track assessment, without proper review or a clear idea of the objective to be served, and often in a manner which removes people's opportunity to choose how they should be cared for, or to continue to cope by themselves while they still can. If our ordinary services could be provided in a more flexible, imaginative, multi-disciplinary way, it would be much easier to fit in appropriate help for people with particular needs.

Below, we summarise what some of these shortcomings are and how they are accentuated for elderly members of ethnic minority groups:-

Housing
The government's own discussion paper, *Growing older*,[2] cites the evidence of serious housing need among Britain's elderly population in general. Lack of basic facilities, poor state of repair, vulnerability to vandalism and burglary, and unsuitability for frail and disabled people are problems so common that they have long since ceased to be 'news'. Immigrant elders are, however, worse off because:

1. They are concentrated in inner city areas where the quality of housing stock is much lower than the general average.
2. Those who have come into this country as declared 'dependents', for whom a sponsor takes responsibility, may not be considered eligible for any help from the housing department (see p 41).
3. The breakdown of 'the extended family' in the very different physical climate and social situation of the United Kingdom can

create acute tensions in shared housing and necessitate separate provision of housing at a late stage in life.

4. Particular needs in terms of easy access to places of worship, food shops etc., risk of racial harassment, and language difficulties, may make it essential that elderly people from a particular ethnic group are rehoused in a particular area.

All these factors generate a need for sheltered housing with warden and community support for elderly members of ethnic minorities. Such sheltered housing demands the appointment of wardens of the same ethnic background as the residents, and ways in which such provision can be made on a group basis need very careful thinking through by housing departments, housing associations and the relevant community groups.

Health services
The health services in general are not well geared to meet the needs of elderly people. Individual practitioners from the various professions are often excellent, but overall the tendency is to grudge the time, trouble and resources needed to give elderly people genuinely equal treatment. Many GPs take little interest in their elderly patients and may indeed take them off their list if they need too much help. The acute wards of hospitals are often not geared to maintain elderly patients' physical and mental functioning at optimum level, so that the trauma of admission for treatment or an operation can be compounded by unnecessary confusion, incontinence and immobilisation. Geriatric and long-stay wards are usually in the oldest sections of the hospital building, and are often relegated to another site, away from facilities and consultant supervision. The prestige of working with the elderly is low and it is one indication of racism in the National Health Service that—from consultants to nursing auxiliaries—an unusually large proportion of this workforce is of Afro-Caribbean and Asian origin. For elderly people living in the inner cities the position is even worse. As the Black Report has shown,[3] health services of all kinds are inadequate and overstressed, and here again, if a choice has to be made in the allocation of resources, the elderly will lose out.

Older members of ethnic minority groups suffer all these disadvantages; they also encounter additional barriers in terms of access because of racial prejudice, cultural insensitivity and language differences. Because health care is so personal, so important to the sick person, and so bound up with understanding of and attitudes to both body and mind, it demands greater sensitivity and more careful communication than any other service. In fact, because of the way in which the health professions have developed and the service is administered, sensitivity and communication are often minimal. This is an enormously complex subject which can only be touched on in this report. Its main importance in this context is that it is essential, not only to improve the way in which mainstream services are provided, but also to make a really conscious and sustained effort *to take services to the users* so that they can talk about their health needs with professionals and receive advice, and in some circumstances treatment, in a place which is safe, familiar and sympathetic. This means that health, social services and voluntary organisations *must* get together to provide outreach health services in clubs, day centres, temples and other meeting places and to improve access to institutionalised health care.

Recreational clubs and day care centres
In some ways, this is the best-provided part of our services because recreational clubs and day care centres have proliferated over the last twenty years. A recent study in just one London borough lists no less than 123 of them.[4] Some are run by voluntary organisations such as the WRVS, Age Concern and so on; some run themselves with their own committee, and in some cases a local authority-paid warden or organiser; others are run by churches with volunteer help; and some are fully-funded and run by the local authority social services department. However, this abundance of provision conceals a basic absence of thought-through policy. If funding has been traditionally provided by the local authority, it usually continues without any serious consideration as to whether it is still justified. Services provided by the local authority itself may be even less questioned in terms of the need which they are meeting, or the extent to which the service enhances the self respect, enjoyment and independence of the consumers. Consistent thinking about gaps in service provision is rare, and there is no clear demarcation between social services' responsibilities and those of the leisure or recreation department (in shire counties these responsibilities are split not only between two departments but also between district and county councils). There is also no clear guideline about what kind of voluntary service should or should not be considered eligible for mainstream funding.

When ethnic minority groups start to compete for premises and funds in order to establish a day care centre in which their members feel welcome and at home, they therefore find themselves hacking their way through a jungle of confusion. However, some points are clear:

1. In view of the proliferation of day care and club provision for indigenous elderly people, ethnic minority communities have a moral right to support in setting up services where their elderly members can feel relaxed and at home and have their special needs met in terms of language, food, religious facilities, sexual segregation and favoured activities.
2. Equitable use should be made of existing community centres and other facilities; they should be made available to ethnic minority organisations and such organisations should not encounter hostility and discriminatory treatment.
3. Appropriate provision for the main ethnic groups will still leave members of smaller communities or those who prefer to use non-segregated services out of account. Help for specialist services should therefore be accompanied by a consistent effort to ensure that generalist services are welcoming and sensitive to the needs of every one who might wish to use them.

Domiciliary support and care
Home help services, meals-on-wheels, sitting-in schemes, and other forms of domiciliary support have proliferated over the last thirty years with very little serious thought about the objectives and efficiency of the services offered.[5] Services have grown or been cut back and have changed their character and their rationale according to the availability of money for particular purposes, technical development, and the enthusiasms or dislikes of particular officers. No authority has worked out a really coherent philosophy of domiciliary care provision, though most pay lip service to it as a basic plank in their provision for elderly people. But if we have little clear thinking about present services, we know even less about effective ways of meeting the growing demand for domiciliary support by elderly immigrants. Chapter 6 in this report indicates that this is an area of growing, and as yet almost totally unmet, need. We must work urgently with the various ethnic groups to devise acceptable means of providing domiciliary support services so that they can be developed, tried and tested before the many settlers now in their sixties and early seventies become very old.

Information, advice and counselling services
Access to competent and trusted information, advice and counselling is not a need which is confined to elderly people or to any particular ethnic group. Indigenous elderly people have many difficulties in this regard, but they are at least likely to have access to sources of

information which they can read and informants whose language they can speak, and they will probably be able to produce the kind of documents which modern bureaucracy demands when making any contact with its services. Elderly settlers, however, may not be literate either in English or in their mother tongue; they may speak little or no English and their birth, marriage or work documentation may be unacceptable to officialdom. There is no doubt that there is a tremendous hunger for help through the bureaucratic jungle and virtually all the day centres and clubs described in this report also function as advice centres. As with so many of the other issues raised in this report, the needs must be tackled on a wide variety of fronts. Better language classes will open up access to standard advice-giving facilities; better interpreter and translation services will enable language barriers to be bridged; better employment practices will increase the likelihood of an advisor with the relevant language skills being available in both statutory and voluntary advice services and will also encourage their use by members of the minority groups. Use of the ethnic press and properly translated leaflets will promote knowledge of welfare rights; outreach to and training of people in the minority groups who have a formal or informal advisory role will improve the quality of service which they can offer; and mainstream funding of specialist advice services for ethnic minority groups to run for their own members will create a trusted and stable resource.

Education and library services
CPA has already done much to document the very poor take-up by all elderly people of educational opportunities, the lack of serious large-print literature and the failure of many library services to offer effective outreach to residential homes or to clubs and day care centres.[6] The need for a positive effort to attract and interest elderly people who may have had little formal education, and who may have hated what they had, cannot be over-emphasised. However, educational and cultural facilities are not only a means to a creative and fulfilled retirement, but also a necessity of life when they enable language barriers to be broken down and a bridge to be built between past and present environment. Again and again the visits made in the course of preparing this report brought out the practical and emotional importance of having access to the literature and current publications of the country of origin, and the opportunity to practise and teach traditional skills and crafts.

It is evident that the library and education services are barely beginning to meet the demand and that there is an urgent need to attract teachers and aides from the ethnic minority groups who may lack formal qualifications but who can help elderly people of both sexes to learn in a reassuring and acceptable way. This is particularly important for elderly women who are most likely to have had little or no formal education of any kind and whose home-centred life may have given very little opportunity to pick up even a smattering of English. If these people are to be enabled to acquire enough of the language to move freely in their new homeland, a much more radical approach needs to be taken to considering and supplying their educational needs.

Local authority policy and practice in relation to multi-racial communities

The previous pages summarised the main issues and needs in service provision for elderly people in general and elderly members of ethnic minorities in particular. How aware are the service providers of these needs and what are they trying to do to meet them? This question needs to be considered from two standpoints: that of eliminating racial and cultural discrimination in all forms of service provision, and that of the special needs of elderly people. There is clearly a very long way to go in both respects. Section 71 of the Race Relations Act, 1976 states that

'Without prejudice to their obligation to comply with any other provision of this Act, it shall be the duty of every local authority to make appropriate arrangements with a view to securing that their various functions are carried out with due regard to the need—(a) to eliminate unlawful racial discrimination; and (b) to promote equality of opportunity, and good relations between persons of different racial groups.'

Ken Young, writing in 1982[7] comments that 'this new duty is however general, ambiguous, and supported neither by sanctions nor incentives. Its interpretation has yet to be tested in the courts and the sole advice to emanate from the central departments merely noted that its effects "would clearly differ from area to area and as between different local authority functions" '.[8] Young goes on to say that when he investigated the efforts of forty or so major urban authorities to adapt policies and practices to the multi-racial nature of their communities, he found that they fell into four broad categories:

The *pioneers*—a small group of authorities, largely London boroughs who have 'proved highly innovative in the face of the stimulus of needs and demands from their multi-ethnic populations and who have been the first to create new committees, new posts, and new machinery and indeed to redefine the norms of policy development in a local authority.'

The *learners*—a sizeable and apparently growing group of authorities where leading figures in the majority party, in association with some chief and senior officers, have accepted the view that major adaptations to policy have to be made. 'As yet, however, little has been done to "flesh out" a generalised commitment with the substance of policy'.

The *waverers*—authorities where councillors and officials 'concede that the presence of a substantial minority population is a significant factor of local life, raising questions about current provision, but believing that for political, or legal reasons or financial reasons the dilemmas are beyond their powers to resolve'. This, Young says, is quite possibly the largest of the four groups.

The *resisters*—these comprise a significant number of authorities with large black populations who appeared to maintain 'a steadfast and unquestioned denial that their presence has *any* implications for local authority provision'.

There has certainly been some progress since 1982 but as the recent report by the Association of Directors of Social Services indicates, any response to service provision in a multicultural society is still extremely ad hoc and patchy.[9] It is not possible to detail here the interesting initiatives to 'sensitise' services for ethnic minority members of all age groups—for example, social worker recruitment, interpreter and translation services, specialist research/development teams, and built-in consideration of the 'ethnic dimension' at the planning stage. For information on these and many other initiatives, local authorities are urged to consult LARRIE, the recently set up Local Authority Race Relations Information Exchange (see Appendix 2 for details of organisations mentioned in the text).

What of services specifically intended to meet the needs of elderly people in ethnic minority groups? A pilot study for this report written in 1982 looked at the level of interaction between such people and the social services departments in two contrasting areas with a large population of well-established and varied ethnic minority groups—the town of Bedford and the Chapeltown area of Leeds.

This was followed up by brief visits to a number of Midland towns. The title of the resulting report was *Out of sight—out of mind* which sufficiently describes its findings.[10] Many authorities were evidently becoming uneasily aware that the social services needs of the minority communities were not being met and that the specialised needs of older Afro-Caribbean and Asian people in particular were rapidly becoming more acute as the immigrant generation grew older and traditional support networks broke down. Even if this awareness was allowed to surface, however, virtually nothing was being done about it. Hard-pressed social services officers took refuge in comfortable phrases like 'they look after their own' or 'of course, they have got the extended family', or more frankly, 'we have an almost total lack of contact with elderly people from the ethnic minorities. We've got far too much to cope with as it is and if they don't come knocking on our doors we leave well alone'. And it was obvious that elderly settlers were not in fact knocking on social services doors. Take-up of day care, domiciliary or lunch club facilities by members of any minority community was virtually nil, as was their contact with welfare rights or information services.

Since then some authorities have begun to make a serious attempt to look at the needs of older members of ethnic minority groups in the context of a general review of their service provision for elderly people, or have set up a special inter-disciplinary group to examine the ethnic dimension and to consult with the communities concerned about their own views of their needs. The London Boroughs of Brent[11] and Haringey[12] and Nottinghamshire[13] and Leicestershire[14] County Councils provide examples of such development. In a few places improvements in service provision have taken place such as the Stroke Club in Birmingham (p 72), Brent meals services (p 107), the local authority funded purpose-built Calabash Centre for Afro-Caribbean elders in Lewisham and local research studies in Nottingham[15,16] but such initiatives are few and far between. In general, any attention which is focused on the ethnic minorities by either health or social services is directed at the younger generation. Elderly people, along with mentally ill, mentally handicapped and physically disabled people, are at the end of the queue for professional interest, and there is no statutory responsibility for their care. It is, therefore, not surprising that those in ethnic minority groups have become, as it were, doubly invisible.

And what of the role of central government? It is greatly to the credit of the Department of Health and Social Security (DHSS) that it commissioned this report and gave CPA a totally free hand in writing it. The Department, through its Social Work Service, has also done a good deal to promote the improvement of services at local level and has held conferences and seminars to encourage the spread of good practice in multi-cultural service provision. The Home Office has undertaken a major review of its funding of specialist staff through Section 11 of the Local Government Act 1966 and has considerably widened the scope of this provision with incidental benefit to elderly people (see p 141). But Section 11 money is still restricted to New Commonwealth settlers and many feel that this does not make sense—the needs of refugees from Eastern Europe or Indo-China, for example, are just as serious. The Department of the Environment (DOE) has published a report *Local authorities and racial disadvantage* which looks at local authority responsibility under section 71 of the Race Relations Act 1976 in relation to such matters as organisation, employment practices, training and service delivery.[17] Also its responsibility for the distribution of urban aid funding has brought it into immediate touch with many of the issues and community organisations concerned in this field. (As Chapter 8 describes it has recently published a perceptive study of projects which it has funded[18]). In general, however, the fear of justifying increased expenditure has meant that no *authoritative* central government guidance has been given to either health authorities or local government on the steps that should be taken to improve the level and quality of their services to ethnic minority groups; and as the summary of implications for action at the end of each chapter in this report indicates, there is room for a great deal of action.

However, it is aspects of positive government policy rather than its inaction which give most cause for concern. Thus, the loss of GLC funding will imperil many of the clubs and day centres set up by ethnic minority groups to help their elderly members which are described in this report. Similarly, arbitrary changes of policy in Manpower Services Commission funding and the availability of urban aid endanger existing initiatives and choke the growth of new ones. Perhaps most serious of all, however, is the effect of the current rules on immigration.[19] These permit elderly parents of people already resident in the UK to be admitted only if they are already wholly or mainly financially dependent on their children in Britain and have no close relatives in their own country to turn to. These conditions are themselves onerous enough. But still more important is the related requirement that the adult child who sponsors such elderly parents 'must be able and willing to maintain and accommodate his dependants without recourse to public funds in accommodation of his own or which he occupies himself'. And he is likely to be asked to swear an affidavit to that effect. As is noted later (see p 41), this clause has the effect of creating a group of elderly people in this country who are utterly without statutory rights to housing, or financial benefits, and if they ask for such help they can jeopardise their sponsor who will have broken his oath and thus committed a legal offence which can render him and his dependants liable to deportation. This condition would be a public scandal at any time: it is intolerable to have a group of elderly people in the country who may starve or die of exposure because they cannot ask for help. It is even more intolerable in a time of recession when, with the best will in the world, the sponsor may be unable to fulfill his commitments.

Conclusion
This introduction has summarised very briefly the plight in which elderly settlers find themselves and the difficulties they have in making use of services as they are at present provided. The rest of the report tries to indicate not only how much there is to be done but the immense potential there is for doing it through a real partnership between the statutory authorities, the ethnic minority groups and the established voluntary organisations. There is no single solution and no simple solution. As the report emphasises again and again, this complex, multi-faceted situation needs to be tackled at many different levels and in many different ways, but it must be done. The quality of service which we can offer to elderly members of ethnic minority groups is a measure of the quality of service which we offer to our elderly population as a whole. To quote CPA's 1982/83 Annual Report 'The prime objective is to formulate and promote social policies which will enable everyone to live their last third of life as fully as possible. We are thus concerned with making all facilities and services more accessible and with promoting specialist services ... The fundamental touchstone is what older people themselves want and need, not what others think is good for them'. If that basic principle can be honestly and courageously pursued, 'triple jeopardy' will become a thing of the past.

REFERENCES
1. Frank Glendenning (ed), *The elders in ethnic minorities*. Beth Johnson Foundation in association with the Department of Adult Education, University of Keele and the Commission for Racial Equality, Stoke on Trent 1979.

12

2. Department of Health and Social Security, *Growing older*, HMSO 1981.
3. Department of Health and Social Security, *Inequalities in Health*, report of a research working group, DHSS, London, 1980.
4. Dianne Norton, *Leisure and elderly people in Lewisham*, Centre for Policy on Ageing, London, 1984.
5. Rodney Hedley and Alison Norman, *Home Help: key issues in service provision*, Centre for Policy on Ageing, London, 1982
6. Eric Midwinter, *Age is opportunity: education and older people*, Centre for Policy on Ageing, London, 1982.
7. Ken Young, An Agenda for Sir George: local authorities and the promotion of racial equality, *Policy Studies*, vol. 3, part 1, July 1982, pp 54–69.
8. Department of the Environment, *Race Relations Act 1976*, Circular S4/77 June 1977.
9. Association of Directors of Social Services, *Social services and ethnic minorities: report of questionnaire survey on social services departments and ethnic minorities*, ADSS, Taunton, 1983.
10. Alison Norman, *Out of sight—out of mind*, Centre for Policy on Ageing, 1982 (unpublished).
11. London Borough of Brent, *Services for the ethnic minority elderly boroughwide*, Report no 114/83 to Social Services Committee, 26 October 1983.
12. London Borough of Haringey, *Report of the ethnic elderly working party to the ethnic minorities joint consultative committee*, November 1981.
13. Personal communication.
14. Leicestershire County Council Social Services Department, *Services for the elderly: a strategy paper presented to the Social Services Committee*, 21 December 1983.
15. Stewart Berry, Mike Lee and Sue Griffiths, *Report on a survey of West Indian pensioners in Nottingham*, Nottinghamshire County Council Social Services Department Research Section, January 1981.
16. Ros Lalljie, *Black elders: a discussion paper*. Nottinghamshire County Council Social Services Department Research Section, 1983.
17. Department of the Environment, *Local authorities and racial disadvantage:* report of a joint government/Local Authority Association working group, HMSO, London, 1983.
18. Stuart Elliott, Graham Lomas, Alan Riddell, *Community Projects Review: a review of voluntary projects receiving Urban Programme funding*. Department of the Environment, London, 1984.
19. Home Office, *Statement of changes in immigration rules laid before Parliament on 9 February 1983 under section 3(2) of the Immigration Act 1971*, HMSO, London, 1984.

2 Immigrant elders: who they are and why they came

Introduction

Although this report is primarily concerned with service delivery here and now, it is important to begin by describing some of the groups we are concerned with in terms of their numbers, why they came, what sort of background they came from, where they settled, what has happened subsequently, and what is known about their current needs and problems. It is only too easy to forget that not only is each immigrant group, or sub-group, distinct in its own particular culture, but it also may consist of different 'waves' of settlers who arrived for different reasons and may have had very different life experiences both before they came and after they arrived.

It should also be noted that for refugees who have fled from political, racial or religious persecution there is an added dimension of loss and fear. People who have lived through terror and torture and barely escaped with their lives are likely to be scarred for life. They may have successfully established homes and careers and families in their new homeland, but in old age all too often the past re-asserts itself and elderly ex-refugees may often experience psychic flashbacks to their traumatic experiences. They may fear, not so much death itself, as having their bodies treated like those in the casual dehumanised holocausts they witnessed in Hitler's concentration camps, or Amin's massacres, or the horrors of Indochina. These ex-refugees may need a very special kind of understanding and support in their old age which neither the statutory nor the voluntary agencies are at present geared to provide. We need much more research to pinpoint the effect which experiences like this have on people's lives and the kind of help which will be of use when health and learned language skills begin to fail. This is a fourth dimension of the triple jeopardy described in this study.[1]

This chapter can do little more than point up the complexity of the scene for a few of the major 'umbrella' groups. It cannot spell out the richness and complexity of the numerous other ethnic minorities which are part of the British population, but it must be emphasised that the problems which older members of these communities may be facing are even more serious, simply because their numbers are relatively small, and awareness of their particular needs and the means to meet them is even less adequate. The space devoted to the

Table 1. People of middle-age and pensionable age usually resident in the UK by country of birth (thousands)

	All persons		Males		Females	
	45-pens. age	of pens. age	45-pens. age	of pens. age	45-pens. age	of pens. age
All countries of birth	10 526·8	9459·0	5862·8	3155·2	4644·1	6303·7
United Kingdom	9667·9	9063·2	5384·4	3016·9	4283·5	6046·3
Irish Republic (incl. Ireland part not stated)	223·0	132·0	122·1	43·8	100·9	88·3
Old Commonwealth[1]	30·2	21·3	16·7	7·1	13·6	14·2
New Commonwealth						
East Africa[2]	14·7	1·6	8·1	0·5	6·6	1·1
Rest of Africa[3]	6·2	1·1	4·4	0·5	1·8	0·6
Caribbean[4]	101·3	16·2	59·1	5·6	42·2	10·6
Bangladesh	9·4	3·8	8·0	0·4	1·3	0·2
India[5]	104·0	44·1	61·4	15·6	42·6	28·5
Far East[6]	12·5	3·9	7·0	1·1	5·5	2·7
Mediterranean[7]	9·4	3·7	5·7	1·2	3·7	2·6

Pakistan	33·7	4·8	22·9	2·1	10·8	2·8
European Community	104·0	41·8	147·7	56·5	66·6	32·9
Other foreign[8]	183·5	113·5	110·2	46·7	73·3	66·8
Total born abroad	858·9	395·8	478·4	138·3	380·6	257·4

1 'Old Commonwealth' includes Australia, Canada and New Zealand.
2 'East Africa' includes Kenya, Malawi, Tanzania, Uganda and Zambia.
3. 'Rest of Africa' includes Botswana, Lesotho, Swaziland, Zimbabwe, Gambia, Ghana, Nigeria and Sierra Leone.
4. 'Caribbean' includes Barbados, Jamaica, Trinidad, Tobago, West Indies Associated States, Other Caribbean Commonwealth, Belize and Guyana.
5. 'India' includes Sri Lanka.
6. 'Far East' includes Hong Kong, Malaysia and Singapore.
7. 'Mediterranean' includes Cyprus, Gibraltar, Malta and Gozo.
8. 'Other foreign' includes 4500 people aged 45 + born in Portugal, 14 800 born in Spain, 11 500 born in the Middle East, 24 700 born in the USA, and 33 500 born in what is now the USSR.

Source: Census 1981, *Country of Birth: Great Britain*, Table 2, 'Country of birth by age by sex', HMSO, 1983.

groups which are discussed is uneven. This is because, although this report is concerned with the needs of *all* elderly immigrants, the Irish are by far the largest group, and there is no doubt that racial prejudice makes the position of people of Afro-Caribbean and Asian origin especially difficult. It seemed important, therefore, to give most space to these communities so that they can speak for themselves about their needs and problems.

The statistical picture

Table 1 shows the numbers of people born outside the United Kingdom who are already of pensionable age or will become so within the next twenty years. This does not give a wholly accurate reflection of the numbers of older members of ethnic minority groups, since a substantial number of people of British origin have been born abroad and there are established ethnic minority groups in this country whose elderly members were born here. However, for the present generation it does give a rough and ready picture of the situation. It will be seen that Irish immigrants are by far the largest group from a single country, with 132 000 people of pensionable age and 223 000 in the middle-age group (45–65). It seems likely that the next largest group consists of various countries in Eastern Europe (see p 35). The figures given for the New Commonwealth countries of origin lump together diverse cultures, languages, faiths and life experiences, but it is important to note the 44 000 people from the Indian subcontinent (with Sri Lanka) who are already of pensionable age and the 104 000 who will become so within the next twenty years; also the 16 000 and 101 000 people from the Caribbean in these respective age groups. These totals alone should drive home the necessity of making proper provision for the many people of New Commonwealth origin who are now growing old.

Useful as these figures are in giving an overall picture, it is the age breakdown and ethnic composition of the population in particular areas which is of key importance. In some inner city wards the 'ethnic minorities' are in fact in a majority and the numbers of older people at risk may be very considerable. It is therefore important that local authorities obtain detailed breakdowns, ward by ward, of the ethnic identity of the residents. The only data at present available for this detailed breakdown is based on tables showing the composition of households by birthplace of the head of the household—the breakdown being by age, sex and whether the individual concerned was born inside or outside the UK (without giving place of birth). These figures do not reflect the ethnic composition of the population very accurately, since they include people of UK descent who were born overseas and they exclude non-Anglo Saxons who were born in the UK and are running their own households—the younger the age group in question, the more inaccurate they become. For middle-aged and elderly people, they are probably reasonably correct, but it seems likely that they underrate the numbers of immigrants from the New Commonwealth and Pakistan. Table 2 below compares data available on individual place of birth, as shown in Table 1 (not available for detailed geographical breakdown) with data available as a result of classification by birthplace of head of household. It will be seen that in all but two cases the former is the greater—the exceptions being East Africa and the Mediterranean (which includes Malta and Gibraltar, as well as Cyprus). The reason for these exceptions is not clear, but they probably reflect in some way the very considerable number of people of UK descent who were born in East Africa and the Mediterranean area between the two World Wars.

Table 2. Country of birth

	Individuals in all types of accommodation by country of birth (thousands)		Individuals in private households where the head was born overseas and who were themselves born overseas (thousands)	
	45-pens. age	of pens. age	45-pens age	of pens. age
New Commonwealth				
East Africa	14·7	1·6	16·0	5·2
Caribbean	101·3	16·2	98·0	14·8
Bangladesh	9·4	3·8	9·2	0·5
India	104·0	44·1	93·0	33·4
Far East	12·5	3·9	10·6	3·2
Mediterranean	9·4	3·7	24·0	9·1
Pakistan	33·7	4·8	32·6	4·2

Source: Census 1981, *Country of Birth: Great Britain,* Table Two and Table Three, HMSO, 1981.

18

Table 3.   Numbers of people of pensionable age (60/65+) born outside the UK, living in households whose head was born in the New Commonwealth and Pakistan by local authority in which the total exceeds 500

	E. Africa	Caribbean	India	Bangladesh	New Common. (other)	Pakistan	Total
Greater London							
Barnet	234	84	555	6	494	45	1418
Brent	430	929	853	5	352	66	2635
Bromley	16	63	297	3	109	25	513
Camden	18	144	235	27	539	25	988
Croydon	133	271	764	10	175	63	1416
Ealing	283	265	1358	4	264	106	2280
Enfield	73	126	246	7	549	14	1015
Greenwich	44	72	309	–	106	25	556
Hackney	21	836	252	8	400	17	1534
Hammersmith	24	350	201	5	193	19	792
Haringey	74	572	369	5	1104	18	2142
Harrow	338	74	497	4	136	46	1095
Hillingdon	61	20	323	–	71	26	501
Hounslow	202	65	671	3	153	73	1167
Islington	16	361	135	6	717	10	1245
Kens/Chelsea	26	215	259	9	217	30	756
Lambeth	59	1092	384	5	438	47	2025
Lewisham	27	521	236	2	190	13	989
Merton	49	134	375	4	138	56	756
Newham	160	282	512	5	104	49	1112
Redbridge	138	65	356	1	110	53	723
Southwark	21	444	105	5	373	15	963
Tower Hamlets	8	198	75	101	206	6	594
Waltham Forest	45	207	186	7	170	63	648
Wandsworth	116	628	488	10	295	52	1,589
Westminster	21	314	252	10	382	31	1,010
Metropolitan Districts							
Manchester	46	362	224	5	102	89	828
Birmingham	181	1174	1327	60	138	344	3224
Coventry	82	63	531	7	50	31	764
Sandwell	21	177	530	7	24	16	775
Wolverhampton	33	289	643	2	20	16	1003
Bradford	35	67	359	15	26	169	671
Leeds	33	209	326	7	82	47	704
Shire counties							
Leicester	491	149	1311	6	55	25	2037
Nottingham	13	280	145	–	28	59	525

Source: Jonathan Barker, *Black and Asian Old People in Britain*, Research Perspectives on Ageing, Age Concern, 1984, using data from the 1981 Census, *County Reports*.

Jewish immigrants
For the purposes of this study, the first big immigration that we are concerned with was that of Russian-Jewish people who arrived between 1881 and 1914 as refugees from the anti-semitic policy pursued by the Russian state after the assassination of Tsar Alexander II. This generation of settlers, highly distinctive in terms of language and culture, has now almost died out, but their patterns of settlement, and the culture inherited by their British children, who are now themselves elderly, remains an important feature in the Jewish elderly population. A second wave of almost 50 000 refugees arrived from Germany in the 1930s, but in contrast with the earlier Jewish immigrants they were mainly professional groups, often less tied to their religion, and more versed in accommodating to the non-Jewish world. Both groups, together with refugees from other parts of Europe, were additions to the established community already living in Britain over many generations. There are now estimated to be about 400 000 members of the Jewish community of whom 18·1 per cent are above retirement age. Almost two thirds of the Jewish population live in Greater London.[3] However, there are high concentrations in some areas of other cities such as Leeds, where Jewish immigrants from Russia comprised 12 per cent of the city's population in 1910. The immigrants followed what has been, as we shall see, a very common pattern by settling first in inner cities, especially in the East End of London where housing was relatively cheap and there was the opportunity to work in the clothing trade and other sweated industry. Again following a common pattern, the children of the immigrant generation have moved steadily further afield, tending to leave their parents behind. As a result, the main centres of Jewish settlement in the London area are now in Redbridge, the northern London boroughs and south Hertfordshire, while others have gone south to the stock-broker belt in Surrey. Thus, the membership lists of synagogues in

---

Table 3 opposite, using data from the 'household' table of the 1981 census, shows the areas of highest concentration of people of New Commonwealth and Pakistan origin who are of pensionable age. They include all the authorities with a total population in this category of more than 500. The figures were originally published in Age Concern's research study *Black and Asian old people in Britain*[2] which also includes 29 other districts and London boroughs with a relevant population of 200–500. These figures should be treated as very conservative estimates, not only because of discrepancies within the census data commented on above but also because the returns are probably a good deal less than accurate. It should, for example, be noted that researchers in Nottingham (see p. 25) estimated that the 148 people they interviewed represented only one in seven of the elderly Afro-Caribbeans in the town, while the census figure quoted above gives a total of 280.

the Brixton and Streatham areas show that 85 per cent of members are over pensionable age[4] and the situation in Tower Hamlets is even more extreme. The old people who are left behind—often because they are in local authority housing and cannot easily move—are thus without specific amenities such as kosher butchers and grocers and are living in increasing isolation. The Hasidic sects which practise very strict adherence to orthodox beliefs provide an exception to this pattern. They have many problems in meeting their own social needs, but are still living in multi-generational communities.

The immense amount which the Jewish community has done to meet the needs of their own elderly people will be described briefly in other sections of this report. Here it is important to note that, although the present generation of elderly people often do not differ visibly from the gentile community in terms of language or dress, their demand for specialist services remains high. They demonstrate that the need for separate provision is not only about specific cultural distinctions, but also about the importance of being with people with whom communication is instinctive, and with whom jokes, means of relaxation, fears, hopes and problems are part of a common unspoken language arising from life experience. It thus appears from the Jewish community that the sense of being more comfortable with your own kind persists indefinitely for some people, even when distinct practices have died out. As a senior official of the Jewish Welfare Board said, 'people will still need specifically Jewish facilities, even if they eat bacon and eggs for breakfast'. This Jewish experience is of great importance in considering how long the need for specialist service provision will continue for other communities.

Irish immigrants
Irish immigration into Britain has been taking place since at least the twelfth century. For the purposes of this report, however, we are mainly concerned with the generation who came over in the 1920s and 1930s, arriving at a steady and substantial rate, for the most part from very rural areas, and following the traditional occupations of Irish working-class immigrants, the men in labouring and navvying jobs and the women in domestic service. The 1981 census figures indicate that there are now over 132 000 such immigrants over pensionable age and 223 000 aged 45–60/65, but immigration fell sharply in the sixties and seventies, so that the bulk of the immigrant Irish population is now middle-aged or elderly. The situation is rapidly changing now, however, since the recession in Eire has

resulted in many young people arriving to try their luck in the big cities of England. There is a serious danger that the effort needed to cope with this new influx and prevent past mistakes from being repeated will divert the energies of the Irish community from concern with the increasing needs of the elderly.

It might be thought that, although they are by far the largest immigrant group, the Irish do not warrant inclusion in a study of services for elderly members of ethnic minorities because they have no immediately distinctive characteristics. In fact, however, the generation of Irish people who came to work on the building sites and motorways, or as domestics in hotels and hospitals, before and after the Second World War, do have particular needs and difficulties in their old age. Many, of course, have settled down and established themselves successfully in this country or else have made enough money to return to Ireland and settle there. But some have not been so successful. Building-site work demands mobility, and so many Irish labourers established a lifestyle of moving from city to city and easily became trapped in a vicious circle of prejudice ('No blacks, no Irish' was a common sign on many landladies' doors), insanitary, overcrowded lodgings, escape to the pub, heavy drinking, and difficulty in accumulating money or possessions. These men were commonly employed 'on the lump', with wages being paid by the day in cash, and were thus encouraged to evade tax and insurance in a system of self-employment which enabled their employers to escape any responsibility for the well-being of their work force. Safety precautions were minimal and many workers are now suffering from the effects of industrial accidents, all-weather work without proper protection, and deafness caused by drilling. In middle age, such immigrants are often unable to find work both because they can no longer cope with heavy manual labour and because the recession and greater mechanisation in the construction industry mean that their traditional employment is no longer open to them. At the same time, their lack of proper employment, insurance and tax records, and their very deep suspicion of British bureaucracy, make them reluctant to claim welfare benefits. Their difficulties are compounded, in many cases, by semi-literacy, since many of this generation of immigrants came from small farms which were worked with manual labour, and even basic primary schooling would be interrupted when the farmer needed extra workers. Also the mother tongue of those who came from the West of Ireland was commonly Gaelic and, as we have noted, there is a general tendency for elderly people to lose facility in a learned language in old age. This is probably less of a problem, however, than a brogue, which can be so strong that communication with indigenous English people is extremely difficult.

The difficulties of female Irish immigrants are less visible, but they also frequently experience a sense of isolation and loneliness, being cut off from a home country which has changed out of all recognition since they left, and not feeling that they belong in English society, which often rejects them as somehow having responsibility for the Northern Irish situation. They may also feel cut off from their anglicised children, or be left behind in the inner city when their children successfully establish themselves elsewhere. Mechanisms which may have enabled them to cope with such feelings when they were young and fit may cease to be effective after the trauma of bereavement or illness, poverty arising from unemployment or the strain of caring for a partner who is disabled.

All these potential sources of disadvantage were discussed with frankness and concern at a recent conference on the ageing Irish in Britain's inner cities,[5] organised during an Irish cultural festival. Speakers put particular emphasis on what they described as a high level of both mental and physical ill-health in older Irish immigrants. This they said derived not only from previous work and living conditions, but also from present poverty, inadequate diet (described by a doctor as 'bread, tea, fried foods and sometimes a tin of beans or a packet of biscuits'), very poor quality lodgings, inadequate heating and minimal sanitation. Poor health is often allied to poor medical care in the inner cities, with a greater likelihood of being looked after by elderly single-handed GPs, or doctors who live outside the area of their practice. Because of this, and also perhaps because of their mobility, older Irish people are said to make extensive use of the hospital accident and emergency services, instead of going to a GP, and consequently to miss out on the consistent health care which becomes increasingly important in old age. Mental illness is also a serious risk. Because of the life experiences sketched above, many older Irish men have become chronic psychiatric hospital patients. They are, therefore, particularly vulnerable if large, Victorian psychiatric hospitals are closed without adequate arrangements being made for the housing and support of long-stay patients. Some have become altogether homeless. A GLC report[6] estimates that ten per cent of their sample of 318 homeless people in London were born in Ireland; and members of parliament at the CRAC conference reported a high proportion of Irish in shelters for the homeless in Birmingham and Manchester. In the past, single people could find lodgings, bedsitting rooms and flats to rent from private landlords, but this source of accommodation has dwindled drastically, and what is available at a reasonable price is usually of very poor quality with little privacy, inadequate fire precautions and no security of tenure. Living there causes loss of personal dignity and social stigma.

Those who have accommodation provided by the local authority or housing association are at least housed, but because they have no capital asset to sell, they are trapped in the United Kingdom—there is no way in which they can get accommodation in the Republic of Ireland. The National Mobility Scheme which enables tenants to move from one local authority to another within Great Britain is now being extended to Northern Ireland, but there is no move to take it further.[7] Even when self-contained housing of reasonable quality can be found for these single and rootless men, it is by no means easy to ensure that they can cope with living in it. A lifetime of receiving wages in cash and paying immediately an all-in charge for board and lodging has not prepared them for budgeting to pay bills, while a deep-rooted tradition that housework is women's work can, according to the senior social worker at the London Irish Centre, often result in the accommodation of those who are rehoused becoming squalid.

Awareness of these needs is now developing fast, as the holding of the conference quoted above indicates, and some action is being taken. The Irish Centre in Camden, for example, has plans for a specialist day centre, open on five days a week and catering for up to 35 people at a time. This, it is hoped, will provide 'meals, craft, keep-fit, some nursing and chiropody, counselling, advice and information, social and cultural activities and, above all, companionship in a caring atmosphere'. The Centre's housing association also plans to provide sheltered housing attached to the hostel which it runs in Kilburn.[8] The Catholic churches in the inner cities also provide a great deal of support, although people in the older generation of immigrants have often been brought up in a rigid and simplistic religious tradition which can make it difficult for them to integrate with an English Catholic congregation. For those who no longer have contact with the church, secular sources of advice and support are very important, not only in helping enquirers through the complexities of claiming welfare benefits, getting themselves on to a housing list and straightening out their financial and other affairs, but also in such matters as claiming an inheritance in Eire—a process which requires a knowledge of Irish land law which is not easily available in England, and documentation in relation to past ownership of property which may not be available. The Irish Advisory Service in Brent is one such organisation which combines advice work with advocacy and pressure-group activities.

There thus seems to be no doubt that there is a sizeable group of Irish immigrants who are old and in ill-health, living in the inner cities and enduring social and cultural isolation. European physical characteristics do not by themselves guarantee integration into English society and, in the opinion of the Irish social worker quoted above, many of these men and women are 'as Irish now as the day they left home. Nothing in the new culture has impinged on their lives'. Their special needs deserve as much consideration as those of any other ethnic minority group.

Afro-Caribbean immigrants
It is well known that the great majority of the present generation of elderly people from the West Indies came to the UK in the boom period after the Second World War to earn money in industries which could not attract indigenous labour. Almost all of them originally intended to go home again, but this expectation has now in many cases been relinquished and there are now, as Table 1 shows, over 16 000 Caribbeans of pensionable age in the UK and over 100 000 who will reach that age within the next twenty years.

The general pattern of immigration and settlement is well illustrated by a study by Age Concern of 234 Afro-Caribbeans aged over 55 and living in London and Manchester; the study also included 370 South Asians and 15 Africans.[9] It is not clear how the interviewees were identified, but of this sample one per cent had arrived before or during World War II, ten per cent during 1946–49, 66 per cent in the 1950s, 18 per cent in the 1960s and five per cent in 1970 or later. They are, therefore, long established as British residents, three-quarters of the Age Concern sample having lived in the UK for over 24 years. They are also very stable in terms of domicile; 96 per cent of the sample had lived for more than ten years in the same city and 68 per cent had lived for more than ten years in the same neighbourhood. This stability may arise partly from a relatively high rate of council house occupation (58 per cent of the sample) with only 12 per cent being owner-occupiers. Twenty-two per cent were in housing association or private rented accommodation; and eight per cent were in rented single rooms. As with the other immigrant groups discussed, they tend to be concentrated in the inner cities of the great conurbations. It is, however, important to remember that there are very distinct differences in language, culture and previous experience between people from different parts of the Caribbean, and that someone whose homeland may be 1000 miles away from that of a fellow 'West Indian' may have little in common with him. People from a particular town or island do tend to settle together so that, for example, the Nottingham survey (see below) found only Jamaicans in their sample. But even if the population in a particular area is relatively homogeneous, there will be exceptions, and it is very important, in terms of service provision, that awareness of the plurality of West Indian culture is maintained.

The most detailed information which we have about older Afro-Caribbean people comes from a study carried out by All Faiths for One Race (AFFOR) which compared the social situation and needs of older Asians, Afro-Caribbeans and Europeans in four Birmingham wards,[10] and from a study of 148 older Afro-Caribbeans carried out by the research section of Nottinghamshire Social Services.[11]

The AFFOR study covered 400 people over pensionable age. They were identified by random door-to-door visits in four Birmingham wards which were known to have a high proportion of residents from ethnic minorities. 179 of those interviewed were Afro-Caribbean, 169 Asian and 52 European, but only 27 of the Afro-Caribbean sample were aged over 70. The number of very old people in this ethnic group is evidently still small, though as is discussed further below it will grow rapidly. The Nottinghamshire study did not use random visits to identify interviewees, because the population of Afro-Caribbeans in Nottingham is too scattered to make this practicable. Instead, the researchers asked organisations in contact with West Indians (for example, the Black People's Freedom Movement, West Indian ex-servicemen and Pentecostal churches) to provide the names of people near or past pensionable age. When these people were asked if they would participate in an interview, they were also asked if they knew of other West Indians in their age group. As a result of using this 'snowball' method 148 people were interviewed (24 refused and 89 were not contacted because time ran out). The authors reckon as an 'educated guess' that this represents something like one in seven of the West Indian pensioners in Nottingham.[12] The AFFOR study will be drawn on heavily in other sections of this report to illustrate the need for particular services, but the Nottingham study is used in this chapter because of its extensive use of verbatim reporting and therefore its value in giving Afro-Caribbean people's own view of their situation.

Respondents were asked what they felt to be the difference between the treatment of older people in England and in the West Indies. The authors of the report comment:

'A strong sense of loss pervades the replies recorded to this question—the loss of close family and community ties, and of respect for the older person. Whether the characterisation of life in the West Indies was true at the time these people left, or is true today, is less important than the *belief* that it is so. The replies also carried a strong indication that the community spirit of the West Indies could not be recreated in this country.'

Examples of such responses are:

'*Back home, family will look after you when you are old, but here they are too busy because they all go out to work.*'

'*I didn't know about "pensioners" until I came here . . . we don't call people old. We don't throw people on the scrap-heap.*'

'*In England, when you reach 60 or 65 years old, you become a social problem. No-one cares about you . . . if you ill, that makes it worse. In the West Indies you don't finish at 60 or 65—you are respected. The older you are, the more respected you are.*'

The looser family and community ties in England not only meant less help, but also less company:

'*You get very lonely here . . . the social life is very poor for a West Indian.*'

Many contrasted this view of community and family life in the West Indies with the role of the state in England:

'*In England the government looks after you, but in the West Indies everybody cares for each other, whether relatives, friends or neighbours.*'

'*When I was in the West Indies, people would assist you and not look for pay, but here you have to depend on the DHSS and the social services for any assistance.*'

Over half those over retirement age were receiving supplementary benefits compared with one in five of the retired UK population as a whole. A third of the sample either had no living children or their children were abroad (a finding with very obvious implications for future need for domestic support) but those who had children were either living with them or in close and regular contact. Over half the households were council tenants. The authors go on to report:

'We asked whether there were enough places where retired people could meet: 36 per cent said there were, 53 per cent said there were *not* and 11 per cent did not know. Those who had already retired were more conscious of a lack of meeting places (57 per cent) than those who had not (47 per cent). Further, there was no difference in the opinions of men and women on this question. Those dissatisfied with existing provision made many suggestions about the type of facilities they would like. Many said they would welcome a club or day centre where they could sit and talk with other elderly West Indians—"where you can talk, and can understand each other's ways". Activities suggested were games, handicrafts and, a frequent request, day trips. Some felt quite strongly that choice of activities, and an involvement of West Indians in running such clubs, were vital prerequisites. Finally, the role of such clubs in facilitating a sense of community was pointed out by several people.'

Asked whether they felt that there were particular problems to which they were more subject than white elderly people, 25 mentioned lower pensions, 23 colour prejudice, 11 loneliness and 27 other difficulties, including a feeling of regret over how they might have been treated if they had grown old in the West Indies. The authors comment that perhaps colour prejudice might have been referred to more often if it had been seen as a problem not confined to *older* West Indians:

'We have been facing problems since we can remember . . . we are black, and we are always treated that way.'

Dependence on state benefits other than the pension can feed suspicions that West Indians receive different treatment:

'A West Indian pensioner has more problems explaining why you are here and why you need money. They seem to ask us so many questions.'

Being a claimant can trigger off prejudiced attitudes, and being black can make matters worse:

'*The problem is they don't look on us as people, they look on us as black pensioners. They don't realise that we know we are black, and we are proud to be black. White people my age group is very selfish. They don't think we should even have a bus pass! I hear black people complain about some of the white pensioners who think black people should not have the things that are provided for pensioners.*'

Thus although older Afro-Caribbeans, like older members of other immigrant groups, may in fact still have the support of a much stronger local community than many of the indigenous elderly people who have been left stranded in the inner cities, they also have a very strong sense of isolation, loss and injustice. It comes through again and again in the Nottinghamshire survey, and was expressed in many of the personal contacts made during the writing of this report.

Asian immigrants
The 1981 Census figures already quoted indicate that there are about 45 700 people in the UK who are of pensionable age and who were born in India or East Africa (some of these are, of course, of Anglo-Saxon origin). The same source shows about 4800 people of pensionable age born in Pakistan, and 3800 aged between 60 and 65 who were born in Bangladesh. But, as this report constantly emphasises, there are many Asians in their fifties suffering from ill health and unemployment whose needs are in many ways similar to those of pensioners. The census shows 118 700 people born in India or East Africa and now aged between 45 and 60–65. As has already been noted, global figures of this kind do nothing to indicate the numbers in a particular district or the particular needs felt by people who are as yet relatively few in number, but who may have intense difficulty in obtaining the services which they require. Global figures based on country of birth also do not represent the immense variety of communities which are subsumed under the 'Asian' label. This variety is well illustrated by Vaughan Robinson's account of the findings of a survey in Blackburn carried out in 1977 and 1978. About 1700 households were interviewed to obtain basic information and a much more detailed schedule was completed for 391 households selected on a random basis.[13] The following distinctive groups were identified:

29

Table 4.   The composition of Blackburn's Asian minority (1978)

Group	Households	Percentage
Rural Indian Gujurati Muslims	505	29·7
Rural Pakistani Punjabi Muslims	361	21·2
Urban Indian Gujurati Muslims	149	8·7
Rural East African Gujurati Muslims	140	8·2
Urban East African Gujurati Muslims	95	5·6
Urban Pakistani Punjabi Muslims	94	5·5
East African Gujurati Hindus	74	4·3
Indian Urdu-speaking Muslims	47	2·8
Punjabi speakers, from elsewhere	40	2·3
Indian Gujurati Hindus	40	2·3
Pakistani Urdu-speaking Muslims	34	1·9
East African Urdu-speaking Muslims	24	1·4
All Marathi speakers	23	1·4
Punjabi Sikhs	23	1·4
All Bengalis	18	1·1
Other Hindus	15	0·9
Others	19	1·1
Total	1701	99·8

Source: Vaughan Robinson 'The assimilation of South and East African Asian immigrants in Britain', Table 1 in *Demography of immigrants and minority groups in the United Kingdom*, ed. D A Coleman, Academic Press, 1982.

Note: The author's spelling of 'Gujurati' has been retained here, but is not followed elsewhere in this report.

Vaughan Robinson quotes his own findings and other research to show that each of these groups has strong individual characteristics in terms of their degree of traditionalism and their relationship both to the country of origin and to life in Britain. The distinction between those who come from a very simple rural village life and those who have sophisticated urban backgrounds is particularly important and demands distinctive approaches to service provision.

The variety of cultures and places of origin is compounded by differences between various 'waves' of immigrants. Thus, the Age Concern study already quoted found that of the 270 older Asians interviewed in London and Manchester, the earliest arrivals in this country were seamen and merchants who were already settled here before 1939. These were followed in the fifties by men recruited to work in industry and public services such as transport, while women joined their menfolk in the sixties and seventies. Some elderly people also arrived to join families already established in this country and a few are continuing to do so. In addition, there has been the considerable influx of Asian immigrants from Kenya, Uganda and Tanzania in the sixties and early seventies. These include refugees from Amin's terrorism in Uganda and many of them, whether from Uganda or elsewhere, have had to abandon considerable wealth and property and flourishing businesses. Some were middle-aged or already old when they arrived and many have lost contact with their families or seen them destroyed. These immigrants from East Africa are, of course, an immensely varied group in themselves, but they also often differ in many respects from those who have come to England direct from the Indian sub-continent. The latter, though not driven out by terrorism or fear of racial discrimination, have often been equally forced to emigrate as a result of unemployment, land hunger or particular government measures, such as the flooding of land to create a reservoir.

The opportunities open to the first arrivals who came when the UK economy was expanding and employment easy to come by, were a very considerable attraction, and reports of their success were reinforced by substantial remittances of money. As with the West Indian immigrants, however, the newcomers almost always intended to return home, and that hope is only slowly fading.

The majority of the respondents in both the AFFOR and Age Concern studies were men, perhaps, as the AFFOR study suggests, because Asian women are not allowed to have as much contact with outsiders as men. It would, however, be a mistake to underestimate the size of the population of middle-aged and elderly Asian women. As Table 1 (p 14) shows, Indian women number two-thirds of the male total in both the middle-aged and pensioner categories. At 28 500 and 43 600 this is a very considerable figure, while in the Pakistani population, elderly women actually outnumber the men, though in the middle age group they are less than half the male total.

There is no doubt that many of these women, particularly those from rural backgrounds, are very vulnerable to social iso-lation in this country. Quite apart from traditional limitations on freedom of movement and social intercourse, they may, like elderly Cypriot women, have received very little formal education and be illiterate in their own language, while many elderly people of both sexes have little or no spoken or written English. The Age Concern study found 38 per cent of their sample in this category, but the percentage was higher in the Urdu-speaking community, for women in general, and for people who came to Britain direct from the sub-continent as fiancées, wives or parents of people already in the United Kingdom. These findings have important implications for mode of service provision.

Although Asians are concentrated in the metropolitan counties, their patterns of settlement differ somewhat from those of other immigrant groups, and particularly from those of the West Indians. According to Peach, West Indians were in 1971 overwhelmingly concentrated in London (55 per cent) and Birmingham (13 per cent), while Pakistanis at that time were 22 per cent in London, 16 per cent in Birmingham and 16 per cent in the West Riding conurbation; the Indian population came between the two, with 33 per cent in London and 14 per cent in Birmingham.[14] Evidence suggests that the West Indian distributions have remained fairly stable since the 1971 Census, but the Asian population has grown substantially in the Lancashire textile towns. Cities such as Leicester and Peterborough which were particularly attractive to East African Asians have also experienced substantial growth. In London there has been less concentration of Asian communities in the inner city, compared with other immigrant groups. The General Household Survey of 1977 is quoted by Peach as showing that only 25 per cent of the Indian, Bangladesh and Pakistani population in London were in the inner boroughs compared with 69 per cent of the West Indians. He suggests that this reflects the later arrival date of the Asian population and also perhaps the greater importance of Heathrow airport as a port of entry and source of employment compared with the railway termini for the West Indians.[15]

Another point of contrast with Afro-Caribbeans is that the Asians have made very little use of council housing. This is reflected both in the AFFOR study and the Age Concern survey. Age Concern found 63 per cent of their sample of Asians were owner-occupiers; seven per cent in a rented council property, five per cent in housing association property, ten per cent in privately rented property and 15 per cent in rented single rooms. One consequence is that the Asian population have retained greater opportunity for mobility and the indications are that the 'outward movement' of the more prosperous members of some communities has already begun. For example, a recent report from Leeds[16] says that in the 1970s an increasing number of Sikh families have moved from inner city terraced housing to the northern suburbs of the city. They have often sold their houses to incoming Moslems. It is too early for it to be clear whether movement of this kind within the Asian communities will result in older people being left behind in the inner cities as has tended to happen with Jewish and Cypriot elders, or whether in most cases the older generation will move with the rest of the family.

The social problems of Asians as they themselves see them have been well described in an unpublished Social Work Service study which includes interviews with a number of leaders of the various Asian groups in a Midlands town[17]. This reports that:

'The most pervasive problem, in the view of the majority of those interviewed, was the adjustment to migration which necessitated change in so many aspects. One community leader talked of "the massive impact" of a move to an urbanised Western society. Even after several years in this country, many were thought still to be viewing their environment as strange, alien and sometimes frightening. The splitting of families was a common result of migration and one which led to concern for the welfare of those left behind, particularly in the case of aged parents. Some missed the emotional, psychological and financial support of the extended family, whereas others felt stifled by living at too close quarters in cramped accommodation.

Roles as determined by Asian cultures had to be adapted radically, and this could be particularly difficult for the elderly. In addition, a demoralising factor for many was that they had failed to achieve the economic goals for which the hardship of migration had been endured. Problems accentuated by the stress of migration were seen to include increased marital and family conflict, trouble between generations, mental illness (especially depression) and problem drinking among Asian men. And, unhappiness stemmed not only from what had been lost but also from the necessity to accept some aspects of the new culture which threatened dearly-held Asian values. Many grand-parents and parents, for instance, were gravely concerned by the Westernisation of the children. They saw the personal liberty afforded to white children as being most undesirable in its potential for weakening family and cultural allegiance . . .

Many Asians remarked that they had been unprepared for the degree of racial prejudice they had experienced in this country . . . The current escalation of racial tension . . . was a cause of acute concern and there were frequent references to fears experienced and the ways in which lifestyles had had to be adapted. Many women said that they never went out alone, nor allowed their daughters to do so.

"There is now a fear—we have this skinhead problem. We have to get lifts now if we want to go out."

"There is no way that my husband would let me go out alone" . . .

The difficulties and needs of Asian women were acknowledged and identified by many. Migration had brought with it a host of pressures and it was frequently suggested that women bore the greatest stresses of isolation, loneliness and communication barriers, particularly if they had little or no extended family. Whilst Moslem women were the least likely to seek employment ouside the home, many other Asian families now expected and depended on women to work for wages and this called for adjustments in family structure which for some were hard to make. Rapid social changes of this nature were exacerbated by the rising tide of Asian male unemployment . . .

Although no one interviewed was in a position to offer statistics, their impressions were that acute family conflict, wife-battering, suicide and attempted suicide were all on the increase. Many people suggested that Asian women who became isolated through matrimonial or family breakdown did not always have access to appropriate forms of support. It was thought that for many reasons Asian women were unable to communicate their difficulties and were often unaware or unsure of sources of assistance. References were made to the capacity of Asian women in desperate situations to withdraw into themselves and suffer acute misery, and there was evidence from health visitors that sometimes this reached the dimension of depressive illness . . .

It was clear that many of the elderly . . . suffered from discrimination, poverty and lack of access to resources. Again, their problems were intensified by the difficulties inherent in their being immigrant. In some cases they missed their homeland, lacked companionship, and found cramped urban living in a cold climate hard to adjust to after the physical space and expansiveness of village life in a warm country. There was often mis-match between the reality here . . . and the original expectation of becoming an elder in the Asian society from which they originated. The status of the wise and respected elder, who could count on the traditional services of a daughter-in-law was likely to be demoted to the role of servicing the family by shopping, preparing meals, collecting the children from school and so on. So, living with the family was no guarantee against the loss of status and a devalued role.

Although health visitors had very few elderly on their case loads, they had nevertheless picked up from young mothers with elderly people in the house that, in some instances, there was great unhappiness on both sides. Whilst some middle-aged couples were as a matter of course caring for their elderly parents, they did not expect to be cared for to the same extent by their own children, and could see problems intensifying in the future. And, in spite of the stated norm that elderly people should be cared for by their own family, there were increasing numbers of elderly Asians, perhaps already as many as 100, living alone.

Some of the religious institutions recognised that their organisations were providing a social as well as a religious centre for some of the elderly within the community:

'They will come and pass the day, or sometimes part of it, and talk with other elderly people. And they are able to get food here.'

But not all elderly people were religious or wanted to spend much time in places of worship:

'The approach of some religious institutions can be somewhat harsh and authoritarian—a bit like your English saying: "As cold as charity".'

... Many found the Social Security system incomprehensible and would have been greatly helped by the consistent presence of an Asian language-speaking clerk in the local offices. Community leaders suggested that, because of lack of knowledge, probably less than half the Asian population received all benefits to which they were entitled. The majority of local Asians interviewed were unaware of the very existence of social services. Even the key helpers, referred to above, possessed scant and often incorrect knowledge of the department, and rarely referred a client. There was constant confusion with social security: "Something to do with money" was a common misconception of the function of social services. Where some knowledge existed, it was usually confined to the provision of day nurseries and child minders, often as a result of information obtained from the health visitor.

The role of social workers and the possible help they could offer remained an unknown service to virtually everyone.'

These findings are well supported, both by other research evidence and by the comments made by workers from a wide range of communities and professional backgrounds in the course of this study. And this is just the beginning. We have very few really old Asians as yet and a great many who are growing old. If the situation is already serious for many and desperate for some, it will become much more so in the near future unless some really determined action is taken to provide the right kind of services.

European immigrants
The complexity noted above in relation to Asian and other immigrant groups applies with equal force to those who have come to live in England from other European countries. Not only were there many pre-war and wartime refugees and the 100 000 members of the Polish forces who stayed in Britain after the war, but also Baltic, Polish, Ukranian, Italian, Austrian and German workers who, in a time of acute labour shortage, were actively recruited by the government to work in British industry. Subsequently, almost 20 000 newcomers arrived from Hungary after the abortive 1956 uprising. These wartime and post-war population movements are reflected in the 1981 census figures. The published data do not give a detailed breakdown of immigration from non-EEC European countries by age, but it may be noted that (to the nearest thousand) there were in 1981, 93 000 people born in Poland living in the UK, 36 000 people born in what is now the USSR, 23 000 born in Austria, 14 000 born in Hungary, 5000 born in the German Democratic Republic and 3000 born in Roumania. It seems safe to assume that these people are, in the main, refugees or displaced persons and that the majority of them are now elderly, while some are very old.

The census does provide the age breakdown of people born in EEC countries, Portugal and Spain, and these are shown below in Table 5. To enable a guess to be made as to how many of the 45–60/65 age band are refugees rather than immigrant workers, the 30–44 age band has also been included. It will be seen that, for most of the countries listed, immigration has continued in the 30–44 age group at roughly the same level as in the next age group up, and it is likely that many of these immigrants will retire to their own country, (though the substantial number of pensioners born in France and Italy should be noted). The exceptions are immigrants from

Belgium and Germany (part not stated) whose numbers between 45 and pensionable age are roughly double those in the age groups just below (5000 and 25 000 respectively), and who already number 3600 and 11 200 people of pensionable age. It seems likely that most of the pensioners and at least half the 45–60/65 age group from Germany and Belgium are refugees or displaced persons who cannot return to their country of birth.

Table 5. **Persons usually resident in the UK who were born in EEC countries, Portugal and Spain, by age group (thousands)**

	All ages	30–44	45-pension age	Of pension age
European Community				
Belgium	14·8	2·5	5·1	3·6
Denmark	9·5	2·9	2·2	1·2
France	39·0	9·4	9·2	6·2
Italy	97·8	30·7	38·0	9·3
Luxembourg	0·4	0·1	1·0	1·0
Netherlands	23·8	7·1	6·7	3·1
Germany, Fed. Rep. of	92·8	14·2	14·4	5·9
Germany (part not stated)	83·6	13·4	25·0	11·2
Greece	12·1	3·7	3·4	1·2
Other foreign				
Portugal	16·5	6·2	3·6	0·9
Spain	40·0	15·3	11·5	3·2

Source: Census 1981, *Country of birth: Great Britain,* Table 2, 'Usually resident population: country of birth by age by sex'. HMSO, 1983.

As was pointed out at the beginning of this chapter, refugees suffer a particularly deep sense of loss. Many will have undergone horrific experiences before they arrived in this country, perhaps as the last surviving member of their family. Most of them still retain a deep feeling of homesickness, and many have either never acquired a real facility in spoken English, or having acquired it, have lost it in old age. The sense of exile seems to be particularly strong amongst elderly people from Eastern Europe who come from countries which have been annexed by the USSR—Byelo-Russia, Estonia, Latvia, Lithuania and the Ukraine—or from countries which are under Communist rule—Poland, Hungary and Yugoslavia. But, apart from this, Eastern Europeans may have little in common and, indeed, in some cases there may be historical reasons for bitter antagonism between them. Not only are the languages and cultures of the different national groups completely distinct, but there may be important differences which sub-divide national groups. They may belong, for example, to one of many different Christian denominations—Orthodox, Roman Catholic or Lutheran, while many of the Jewish immigrants discussed above came from Eastern Europe. It is therefore very important that Eastern Europeans should not be assumed to be a homogeneous group when planning any kind of specialist service provision. Up till now, their social needs have been mainly met through licensed clubs where members of each community congregate and where informal help with form-filling and translation can be obtained. In some cases these have become well-established and highly successful enterprises with facilities which attract the younger generation. But, in general, the average age of membership of these clubs is rising and capacity to offer mutual support and outreach to housebound and disabled people is lessening. Moreover, the clubs do not meet the needs of women who do not wish to attend them unaccompanied, and are also unsuitable for those who do not wish—or cannot afford—to drink alcohol.

As was noted above, many of those who came to this country during and after the second world war are now getting very old. For example, of the 930 parishioners of the Polish Catholic Church in Slough (about half the Polish population in the area) over a third are of pensionable age and there were 29 deaths in 1983 compared with a previous top figure of 20. A voluntary worker attached to the church (see Appendix 2) has identified twenty people who are sufficiently disabled to need residential care and seven who are in care. This particular community is doing its utmost to help its own older people and has plans for a ten-place residential home with a related day centre, the latter being based in the social activity area of the recently-completed church. Smaller communities and those in less prosperous parts of the country will, however, have great difficulty in making this kind of provision, and many elderly Europeans live in fear of entering a residential home where they will be unable to communicate with staff and other residents, or else of having to leave the area in order to go into a specialist home many miles away.

Cypriot immigrants
Elderly Cypriots represent a substantial proportion of older New

Commonwealth immigrants. We do not have figures which separate them from people born in Gibraltar, Gozo and Malta, but certainly a very large proportion of the 11 000 people of pensionable age born in Mediterranean countries have come from Cyprus. The nearly 30 000 people in the middle age group indicate that this number will rise steeply. The size of the Cypriot community is all the more marked because the population is concentrated in relatively few areas, primarily in the London boroughs of Haringey, Enfield, Islington, Camden and Hackney. Haringey leads the field with perhaps 30–35 000 people of Cypriot descent (including those born in this country) out of a total borough population of 228 000.[18]

The first major group of Cypriots (mainly Greek-speaking) came during the 1930s when the Cypriot economy was still mainly based on subsistence agriculture. Many parents could not afford to keep their sons at school beyond the age of 12. Girls often received no formal education, and were kept at home to learn social skills, sewing, cooking and home management in readiness for marriage. These first young male Cypriots followed the example of Italian immigrants and settled mainly in the Camden Town and Soho areas. Accommodation was scarce, could only be rented and was often run-down. They were soon joined by sisters or brides who worked alongside their husbands or brothers, or were employed in Jewish dress factories and furriers—the skills acquired for marriage were now used for survival. Most of the Cypriots who came in the thirties never saw their elderly parents again.

Another wave of immigrants, both Greek and Turkish, arrived in the late fifties and early sixties. They came for a variety of reasons— to earn money, obtain education or to escape the new political situation in Cyprus and the problems that independence brought to a small country which had been ruled by outside powers for thousands of years. This time, young couples with children came and were later joined by parents and other members of the family. After the crisis of 1974, these Cypriot residents were joined by thousands of homeless relatives who came literally with only the clothes they stood up in. These refugees included elderly people, some of whom had lived in Britain for over 30 years and had returned to Cyprus to retire, whole families, mothers with children, teenagers and children on their own. Both Greek and Turkish Cypriots fled the country, though the majority were Greek.

In Cyprus elderly people were traditionally cared for by children who usually still lived nearby, though they set up their own household when they married. There was no sudden retirement, and men continued with farming or gravitated to the coffee shops for discussion about local issues on which their opinion was treated with respect, while older women continued to help with childrearing and teach their skills to grandchildren. In England, though many live with their sons and daughters, pressure on housing space may make this difficult or impossible and the outward migration of the younger generation which we have noted in other communities may make it difficult for children to offer traditional support to parents, left behind in the inner city. Again, as in other communities, Cypriot women are more and more forced to work outside the home, and while this may make older people valuable assets as childminders, it also means that those who need daytime care and company may not obtain it as easily as in the traditional setting.

There is a major language problem. Often elderly Cypriots are literate in Greek or Turkish, but cannot cope with spoken English. Some are able to speak English, but cannot read or write it easily, and some elderly women who received little education as children may also be illiterate in Greek and Turkish. There are, therefore, major difficulties in taking up any services or facilities for which spoken or written English is necessary, and this includes many day-to-day activities as well as use of the health and social services. In the absence of close contact with their families, there may be quite intense social isolation, especially for the women whose culture does not allow them to frequent the coffee shops. (This is, in any case, an expensive means of socialising, since refreshments have to be bought and the card games played involve gambling). Older members of the Cypriot community thus share many of the problems experienced by Asian elders described above.

Chinese immigrants
(The account given in this section is based on information provided by Mrs Shu Pao Lim, a Chinese community development worker in the London Borough of Camden's Social Services Department, and by the London Chinese Information and Advice Centre).

The census figures show that in 1981 nearly 137 000 UK residents were born in New Commonwealth countries of the Far East (Hong Kong, Malaysia and Singapore) and of these 12 500 were middle-aged and nearly 4 000 of pensionable age. The vast majority of these people came from the New Territories in Hong Kong where they worked in the fields growing rice, and when that became unprofitable because of dumping by the United States, growing vegetables. Free education was not available in Hong Kong until the 1970s and most families could only afford to educate their sons, and then only until they were twelve years old and able to work. Illiteracy in both Chinese and English is, therefore, very common in the immigrant generation, especially among women. The main group of these immigrants were men who arrived in the 1950s and established themselves in the catering trade. Their wives and older children who could help in the take-away shops and restaurants came in the 1960s, and elderly parents arrived in the 1970s, together with children who had been left behind for the grandparents to look after, or who had been sent back because their parents did not have enough accommodation or wanted to work. The 4000 Chinese elders now in the country may therefore either be original immigrants or people who came in quite recently to join their families. In the latter case, they will be totally unaccustomed to life in England. In either case, there is no doubt that they are quite often in great difficulties, suffering not only from culture shock but also from ill health arising from a lifetime of work in unhealthy kitchens or on the land. They have experienced overcrowding and rejection by the younger generation while lack of work documentation and the perennial language and literacy problem make it very difficult for them to find out and claim their welfare rights (if they have any) or to make use of the health service.

Unlike the members of the other immigrant groups discussed in this report, the Chinese are relatively scattered, apart from long-established communities in dockland areas such as Cardiff, Liverpool and East London. This is because the restaurant/take-away trade requires them to settle in an area where there is no direct competition. The consequence is that all the problems reported concerning other immigrant groups are exacerbated by lack of community support and by the difficulty of providing specialist services to a dispersed population. Intense social isolation for people of all ages is therefore a very common experience, and this is exacerbated by very long hours of work and lack of anywhere except the gambling parlours and amusement arcades of Soho's 'Chinatown' in which to spend leisure. Where a concentration of population does warrant it, there is a great need for small local drop-in centres to relieve the isolation of older people who are no longer fit to work, even if they have not yet reached official retirement age, and those who were brought in to look after grandchildren who have now grown up. Provision required in such centres would be no different from that required by other communities and described in some detail in Chapter 5—facilities for tea-making, video films in their own language, the opportunity to play games without gambling and a comfortable place to sit and chat. For the very scattered families, a mobile advice/teaching/library unit could provide a valuable service.

The vulnerability of older Chinese people may be increased by their lack of entitlement to welfare benefits or assistance with housing. They have perhaps been affected more than any other immigrant group, by the provision in the immigration rules quoted in the introduction to this report, (page 10) which requires someone bringing in dependents after 23 May 1980 to undertake in writing 'to maintain and accommodate his dependants without recourse to public funds in accommodation of his own or which he occupies himself'. This 'undertaking in writing' now usually has to be sworn as a legal affidavit and the provider can therefore be taken to court if he fails to comply—regardless of any changes in his own circumstances. This could mean that he and the rest of his family lose their right to stay in the UK. This fear hangs over many Chinese families with an elderly dependant and may deeply exacerbate family tensions because there can be no escape into separate housing and no financial contribution from the elderly person who can no longer work. There also appears to be no official definition of 'public funds' and this gives rise to fear of using *any* free public service, including the national health service. This situation is complicated still further by the fact that employment in the catering trade often means living in tied accommodation, so that when a job is lost, a whole family can become homeless and, because of high mobility in the trade, it is very difficult for workers to qualify for council housing. Housing conditions for the Chinese community as a whole are therefore probably worse than for any other ethnic group.

It seems extraordinary that with at least 30 000 people of Chinese ethnic origin in Greater London alone, more thought has not been given to the need to improve the access of this community to information and advice, interpreter services, health and social services, and housing. The London Chinese Information and Advice Centre, which was set up as recently as September 1982, is endeavouring to highlight some of the major areas of concern; the Bloomsbury Health District has launched a small-scale investigation of use of the national health service by Chinese people, and a few boroughs have a specialist social worker in post, but initiatives like this are of minuscule proportions in relation to the need (and, as the London

Information and Advice Centre is funded by the GLC, even its continuing existence is uncertain). The particular problems of elderly members of the Chinese community represent, in an extreme form, the uncharted problems and needs of the Chinese community as a whole.

Conclusion

This very brief review of the seven main immigrant groups cannot, of course, do justice to their complexity and as the introduction to this chapter pointed out, it ignores the literally hundreds of others which have a distinct identity in terms of language, culture, history and religion. The point of providing these seven sketches is to illustrate, as far as possible in their own words, the kind of experience which elderly immigrants have undergone, the difficulties they encounter, the strength of their sense of community and the isolation and homesickness to which they may be subject. For, although one of the objectives in writing this chapter has been to illustrate the diversity of older members of ethnic minorities, another is to illustrate the extent to which they have common problems and common needs for particular kinds of service—for the opportunity for social relaxation with their peers, for decent housing, for access to the health service, for help in overcoming the barriers created by language and dietary customs, for educational facilities, entertainment, welfare rights advice and domiciliary support. The following chapters of this report spell out these common needs in more detail and discuss ways in which they can be met.

SUMMARY OF ACTION REQUIRED

(The action listed in this section relates to use of census and other Office of Population Censuses and Surveys (OPCS) data. Action in relation to service provision is discussed at the end of other chapters).

Action by ethnic minority groups

1. Press the local authority to obtain *and to make easily available* the detailed local census data on residents' age and country of birth for wards which have any appreciable immigrant population.
2. Press for the publication of breakdowns of local population predictions by age and ethnic group over the next twenty years.
3. Make use of this data to press for provision of appropriate services.
4. Encourage and help the smaller ethnic minority groups revealed

43

by the census data to investigate and make known the needs of their own members.
5. Publicise the case for an 'ethnic question' in the next census which will give proper data for planning to meet the needs of members of ethnic minority groups born in this country.
6. Use the census data to make those living in wards with a high concentration of ethnic minority groups aware of their voting strength and so obtain political recognition and representation.

Action by local authorities and health authorities
1. Obtain the relevant census data and future predictions of age distribution in the most detailed possible form by ward, age and country of origin.
2. Make the data available in a way which makes it easily understood, including the use of graphs and bar charts, and publicise its availability.
3. Use the data as a basis for a critical evaluation of the adequacy of existing services and equity in distribution of resources, and take appropriate action.
4. Study the data to identify areas of unmet need and unpublished need, especially in relation to small or scattered ethnic minority groups and groups with special needs.
5. Take the data seriously as a base for forward planning to meet the needs of people at present 'middle-aged'.

Action by central government
1. Bring the implications of the data to the notice of service providers and encourage them to plan to meet the particular needs of the major groups in their areas.
2. Ensure that proper use of census data is made in applications for urban aid and other grant applications and assess applications in the light of the evidence presented.
3. Ensure that an 'ethnic identity' question is included in the next census so that a full and fair view of the range and age structure of ethnic minority populations is available as a basis for future planning and a means of ensuring equitable distribution of resources.

REFERENCES
1. Ron Baker (ed). *The psychosocial problems of refugees,* British Refugee Council and the European Consultation on Refugees and Exiles, London 1983.
2. Jonathan Barker, *Black and Asian old people in Britain: first report of a*

44

research study. Research Perspectives on Ageing, Age Concern Research Unit, Mitcham 1984.
3. Jewish Welfare Board Annual Report, London, 1982.
4. Michael Jimack, *Jewish senior citizens in South London: a study of social and community needs,* Central Council for Jewish Social Service, London 1983.
5. Conference on 'The ageing Irish in Britain's inner cities' at the CRAC Festival, Birmingham 1984.
6. Greater London Council, *Sleeping out in Central London,* a report by the Central London Outreach Team, GLC, London, 1984.
7. Personal communication from Donal McGrath, Brent Irish Advisory Service.
8. London Irish Centre, *Annual Welfare Report,* 1983.
9. See ref 2.
10. Anil Bhalla and Ken Blakemore, *Elders of the ethnic minority groups,* All Faiths for One Race, Birmingham, 1981.
11. Stewart Berry, Mike Lee and Sue Griffiths, *Report on a survey of West Indian Pensioners in Nottingham,* Nottinghamshire County Council Social Services Department Research section, January 1981.
12. Ibid.
13. Vaughan Robinson. 'The assimilation of South and East African Asian immigrants in Britain', Table 1 in D A Coleman (ed), *Demography of immigrants and minority groups in the United Kingdom,* Academic Press, London, 1982.
14. Ceri Peach, The black population in Britain 1945–1980 in D A Coleman (ed) *op. cit.*
15. See ref 14.
16. Leeds Community Relations Council Housing Liaison Group, *Race and Housing Associations,* Leeds 1984.
17. Unpublished DHSS Social Work Service Report, 1984. Quoted by permission of DHSS.
18. Susie Constantinides and Fuat Alkan, *Cypriots in Haringey* (undated and privately published). This report, written by Cypriot liaison officers working in Haringey Social Services Department, is also the source of the remaining information in this section.

3 Housing needs and provision

Introduction

The particular housing disadvantages faced by the Afro-Caribbean and Asian communities have been well documented—most recently in Colin Brown's survey for the Policy Studies Institute.[1] In general, the research shows that Afro-Caribbeans and Asians in council properties tend to be put in high-rise flats on unpopular estates, and those who have bought their own houses have been forced by availability and cost to take on old property in poor condition so that upkeep and heating become a constant struggle. The housing shortage in general and in particular the lack of large dwellings in which an extended family can be properly housed create severe overcrowding. Similar problems are experienced by the Cypriots and Chinese and, as has been noted, inadequate housing is a major problem of the Irish population. Those who are old experience the same disadvantages, but they are often compounded by increasing physical disability, family tensions, loss of family support as younger people move out of the inner city, fear of racial harassment and physical assault, and social isolation.

All these pressures have given rise to a strong demand for the provision of grouped flats with warden support to meet the particular needs of older people. It is perhaps ironic, as an unpublished report from Age Concern Greater London has pointed out, that community groups should be putting such a strong emphasis on sheltered housing of this kind as a solution to the housing problems of ethnic minority old people at a time when the general concept of sheltered housing is receiving some criticism. However, sheltered housing does seem to be particularly relevant to the special circumstances of elderly immigrants, and especially those who have lived in a large family group all their lives and do not speak English. Small units can be established in the heart of the community concerned so that familiar shops, and places of worship, are nearby; the extended family members may be able to offer support much more effectively when they are freed from the stresses of living under the same roof; a warden can do much to supplement more traditional kinds of care; and the loss of the extended family group can be made up by the company of a peer group.

Although the need is common to all the communities, it is perhaps felt most strongly in the Asian groups. Atul Patel of Asian Sheltered Residential Accommodation (ASRA) Leicester explains the situation as it affects Asians from the Indian sub-continent in the following terms[2]:

'There is a widely-accepted myth that Asian people in this country (originally from the sub-continent of India) are able to care for their old as well as their young under one roof because of their extended family. However, a number of factors existing in contemporary Britain combine to put severe strain on this family system with adverse effects. The different economic and social structure in this country makes it impossible for married children to shoulder their traditional responsibilities towards their parents—the smaller houses and different lifestyles are examples. Also the middle-aged and elderly are no longer the breadwinners and, with their sons and daughters working, their authority is undermined.

Thus, there is an increasing number of elderly Asians who cannot be accommodated with their families and who feel rejected and unsupported. In addition, there is in Leicester a substantial number of elderly and handicapped refugees from Uganda and other parts of East Africa. They are often victims of loneliness and depression through having lost the community support which sustained them in East Africa and being unfamiliar with the system operating in this country. In this respect, elderly East African Asians are forced migrants from a particularly vulnerable section of the Asian community.'

Particular difficulties also often arise for the many older Asians who have no immediate family in this country and who live as lodgers in another household. Some of these pay very highly for their accommodation, but cannot prove this because their landlord is reluctant to invite questions (especially if it is council property or the mortgage has restrictions on sub-letting) and he may also be reluctant to attract attention from the tax inspector. In consequence, the lodgers cannot include a claim for rent in their supplementary benefit claim and may have to starve themselves in order to pay for their accommodation.

Sheltered housing developments
Asian initiatives
One of the first initiatives taken to try and meet this growing and often desperate need was the ASRA project in Wandsworth where two houses have been converted to provide ten self-contained flats (one for use by a warden). This project was set up by the Migrant Services Unit of the then London Council for Social Services

and community workers at the Millan Community Project in Wandsworth and was funded through two local housing associations. These developments provided a model for further initiatives elsewhere and GLC funding has now been obtained to appoint an ASRA co-ordinator to encourage sheltered housing provision wherever it is needed in the London area. Two further units have already been opened in south Lambeth and nine further ASRA-sponsored applications for Housing Corporation money are in the pipeline, though it is very unlikely that they will all obtain funding. Not all of these follow the Wandsworth model. In Camden, for example, four large houses which adjoin each other are being converted to provide flats designed for elderly people on the ground and first floor, and larger accommodation for families upstairs. This will, it is hoped, enable familes to live above elderly relatives and continue to offer support. The ASRA Lambeth co-ordinator, Gerard Lemos, emphasises that often the real problem is that the whole family needs housing, not just the individual elderly person.

A similar but independent development role is undertaken by another ASRA organisation based in Leicester. This has been in operation since 1980 and already has 35 flats in occupation and another 115 in various stages of development. Some of these are purpose-built blocks where very frail people could be cared for. ASRA Leicester now employs a development officer whose task is to work with, encourage and inform local groups all over the Midlands who want to develop sheltered housing initiatives and help them to make contact with appropriate housing associations. Some twenty such local groups are showing interest and enthusiasm in this field, but they need a lot of help if interest is to be converted into effective action.

In Birmingham, a similar development role has been taken on by a worker, Anil Bhalla, based at the Asian Resource Centre. Anil Bhalla was one of the authors of the AFFOR study which pioneered concern in this field[3] and he is working with three housing associations which have projects in the pipeline. The Midland Area Housing Association has acquired two houses in the Handsworth area to convert to six self-contained units for Asian elders; the Family Housing Association is to build twenty new self-contained units with a resident warden, and the Birmingham Friendship Housing Association is converting a row of large houses in the Sparkbrooke area. This last development will house elders from all racial groups, with each house containing tenants from a particular ethnic group.[4] Anil Bhalla, who has built up his own list of 78 elderly Asians in desperate need of housing will handle all Asian referrals to these projects and, as is reported further below, he has also negotiated successfully with the Anchor Housing Association to obtain preferential use of their sheltered accommodation as it becomes vacant.

In Leeds, the Leeds Federated Housing Association is making available a unit of six flats and bedsitting rooms in the Beeston area of the city for middle-aged and elderly Asian men and is completing a newly-built scheme of six more flats in the Hyde Park area which will also be used for Asian elders. Discussions are under way with a number of agencies, voluntary and statutory, to set up a support system for incoming tenants.

Provision of a rather different kind is offered by Aram House in Romford and Milan House in Southall. These two developments in converted property provide what is, in effect, hostel accommodation for older Asian men, with single or shared bedrooms and a communal sitting-room. Aram House (nine single rooms) does not have a kitchen which is big enough to provide a main meal and this is taken by arrangement in a local cafe. In Milan House (five rooms providing ten places) cooking is done by the warden and volunteers.

Afro-Caribbean initiatives
The Carib Housing Association is as yet the only specialist sheltered housing scheme which has obtained housing association status in its own right as opposed to working through another organisation. It was started by an Afro-Caribbean woman, Mrs Lee Samuel, who when she found herself a widow with no need to work and with time on her hands, devoted her energies to meeting what she saw as an evident housing need. She emphasises that plenty of free time and endless perseverance were necessary to get through the Catch-22 situation in which the Housing Corporation will not register a new association until it has got a project off the ground, and it seemed impossible to get a project off the ground without funding from the Corporation. However, the London Borough of Kensington and Chelsea eventually put up the money to convert a large property in Notting Hill into eleven self-contained bed-sitting room flatlets for elderly Afro-Caribbeans in need of housing. This enabled the process of registering as a housing association to go ahead, and now two new buildings are under construction in Brent and Haringey which will provide a total of 52 one-bedroom flats, while the original project is open and functioning very successfully.

Lee Samuel emphasises the importance of great care in thinking through how the warden should be recruited. The Notting Hill project had difficulty in attracting suitable people, because the right kind of person was already well established in her own home and did not want to move into tied accommodation. The solution has been to employ two people on a split shift system who sleep in when on duty but have their own homes to go back to. The room intended as the sitting room in the warden's flat is used as an office which is of great value in giving residents somewhere to come for help and advice without invading the warden's privacy. This level of provision for an eleven-flat unit is only possible because of a large GLC grant, and it may have to be reduced. In the security of sheltered housing, and with the help of a warden to act as go-between, the association's tenants do make effective use of the home help service.

Lee Samuel takes the view that specialised housing of this kind will only be needed by Afro-Caribbeans for the next fifteen or twenty years to meet the particular needs of the immigrant generation. She believes that the next generation will be very different and will not need separate help. She also takes the view that local authorities should, on principle, not provide separate services themselves, though this is permissible for a voluntary body. These are opinions which would be hotly argued by others.

Cypriot initiatives
The Greek Orthodox church in Haringey has established bed-sitting room units with shared toilet facilities in a group of houses close to the church. Discussion is also going on between the London and Quadrant Housing Association and Cypriot community liaison officers about the provision of ten detached units with a peripatetic warden, and a purpose-built block with 30 units and two wardens, one a Greek speaker and the other able to speak Turkish.

Jewish initiatives
Impressive action to meet the needs of their own older people has been taken by the Jewish community. For example, the Leeds Jewish Welfare Board has four sheltered housing schemes comprising some 120 units and it also has many elderly tenants in ordinary flats on the estate built by the Leeds Jewish Housing Association. Numerous developments also exist in the London area, often in association with a residential care home so that staff in the home can provide a supportive service, but there is a great demand for further development in the area to which the younger Jewish population has moved so that older people can be near their families and have easy access to Jewish shops.

Particular issues relating to specialist sheltered housing
Design features reflecting the customs of a particular community
These are especially important in Asian housing and may include baths which are designed so that the user can pour clean water over himself in the traditional way; deep kitchen cupboards suitable for storage of items bought in bulk such as chapatti flour; and gas cookers (Asian cooking requires a naked flame).

The need for housing to be set within a concentrated population of the relevant community and have communal facilities
There should be a communal sitting room where residents can meet together to watch video, play cards and chat, and which can also be used as a drop-in centre by people not living in the accommodation so that the risk of stigma and isolation is avoided. There is evidence that, although such communal facilities are often unused in sheltered housing occupied by elderly English people, the ethnic minority communities do make extensive and successful use of them and they offer a valuable and valued resource.

The need for much care and skill in the selection, support and training of sheltered housing wardens
This is an area in which major mistakes can be made if the appointment is not carried out in close association with members of the relevant community who have access to the community network and can assess the suitability of applicants. In Leicester, for example, a housing association trying to promote multiracial sheltered housing advertised the post in the normal way and got seven applicants of whom six were white. When the ASRA project leader was called in to advise, they tried again and this time the result was reversed.

The role of wardens in specialist sheltered housing
Wardens may be required to play a much more supportive and enabling role in these sheltered housing units than would be the case in non-specialist provision, because they may be catering for people who have had no previous experience of independent living and who are not able to speak or write English, so that obtaining or using even the most basic services presents serious difficulties. ASRA Leicester lists the tasks such a warden needed to undertake in their first development as follows[5]:

> *Immediately on allocating:* liaising with former landlord (if any) over transition to new accommodation; liaising with the Housing

Association over commencement of tenancy, signing of agreement, keys etc.; sorting out social security and extra needs payments; arranging for utensils, furniture, food, bedding whilst benefit is being sorted out; arranging for community support: neighbours, friends, local shop owners; explaining heating and hot water system; informing utility services.

In the medium term: fixing clothes-lines, coat hooks, shelves; collecting and paying in rent when necessary and trying to avoid arrears; paying gas bills and sorting out overcharging; reading letters and correspondence over rates, DHSS visits, etc.

In the long term: helping relationships between tenants and encouraging them to help each other; getting tenants registered for travel permits; sorting out passport problems; helping to forge links with other residents and community organisations; sorting out recurring minor problems, eg gas boiler, pilot light, light bulbs, and referring other maintenance matters to the housing association; general visits enquiring about health etc as often as necessary; advising/counselling tenants on budgeting, relationships with family, economical use of central heating etc; making referrals to other agencies when necessary.

The warden of the Lambeth ASRA projects—a young male graduate—is not at all the middle-aged motherly type commonly associated with standard sheltered housing. He sees his role as a dual one of warden and community development worker whose task is not only to see that tenants' needs are met and encourage self-help, but also to publicise and explain the concept of sheltered housing to the wider Asian community and encourage interaction between tenants and their neighbours so that social isolation and stigmatisation are prevented. He also feels it is important to encourage families who may feel guilt and shame at the decision of the tenant to leave his previous home to see that this need not entail the loss of their caring role, and that in fact they may be able to help much more effectively when under less stress from their housing arrangements.

The role of housing associations and the Housing Corporation
The amount of money being made available to the Housing Corporation is being drastically reduced and competition between associations for a slice of the cake is correspondingly increased. The more registered associations there are, the tougher the competition; so the Corporation is becoming increasingly reluctant to register

new ones. As we have seen, the Carib Housing Association had a stiff fight to get established, although it was in the field before things had got quite so tight, and ASRA Leicester and ASRA Lambeth are still struggling to achieve registration. They are being assisted in this by the Housing Association Consultancy and Advisory Service which is being paid by the Help the Aged Housing Trust to provide expert help. (The Trust has been extensively involved in both projects since their inception.)

The Housing Corporation's official policy on registering new associations is set out in a report on specialist sheltered housing written by a working group which was sponsored by Age Concern England and the Help the Aged Housing Trust.[6] The Corporation requires the association concerned to show that 'it has a role to play' either because of a lack of associations operating in a particular area or because it proposes to meet a type of housing need not adequately met by existing associations. The working group felt that the Corporation's policy was bland and unrealistic in that it did not take sufficient account of the very strong feelings which some ethnic minority communities have about running and developing their own scheme and the suspicions which arise if they always do this under the wing of a 'white' housing association. The report urges that associations which meet all the Corporation's other criteria should be accepted for registration if no similar ethnic minority housing association is working in the area.

At present, projects of the kind described in this chapter usually result from a community group persuading an existing housing association to develop a project on their behalf and co-operate with them in its management. This is neither an easy nor an ideal arrangement. Housing associations may be sympathetic, especially as the programme manager of the Housing Corporation is on record as stating that the Corporation would consider the housing of elderly ethnic minority groups as a very high priority. Work in this field may therefore improve an association's chances of getting some funding. However, the community group concerned will have no control over the association and no means of making sure that it succeeds in carrying out its undertakings. In these very small-scale projects, failure to achieve just one conversion as planned can have a very damaging effect on the whole programme.

There may also be difficulty in negotiating development and management agreements which are felt to be fair by both parties. The working group's investigation showed that such agreements were the source of a great deal of frustration and suspicion amongst the ethnic minority communities and there was a need to clarify very early in the negotiations exactly what was being undertaken and how it would be funded. The group's report provides very detailed advice and examples of actual documentation on this aspect.

Some housing associations are taking an interest in providing specialist sheltered housing on their own initiative, but they often do not consult the relevant community group members early enough in the planning stage, with the result that serious mistakes in design and layout may be made. Some of the common pitfalls have now been spelled out in Race and housing, a guide for housing associations produced by the National Federation of Housing Associations.[7] Useful though this is, it is no substitute for regular and frequent personal consultation with knowledgeable and experienced people, and this is needed still more at the stage of allocating tenancies and selecting a warden. Putting neighbours together who are compatible in terms of sex, religion and language, for example, can be crucial. The Age Concern/Help the Aged report discusses the general issues and draws attention to the need, and also provides a great deal of practical advice to housing and community groups in setting up schemes for elderly people from ethnic minorities.[8]

Another important issue is the use of housing associations' existing stock to house members of ethnic minorities. In general, the associations are only now waking up to the need to monitor their use of their stock and make sure that applicants from ethnic minorities get an appropriate share. Associations which specialise in sheltered housing may have great difficulty in making contact with potential tenants from the minority groups, unless they are working with members of the communities concerned.

One encouraging development in this field, which could be imitated elsewhere, is an initiative taken by a group of Leeds housing associations in association with Leeds Community Relations Council (CRC), the local authority housing department and the Equal Opportunities Unit of the City Council. They have examined the way in which housing associations communicate with the local communities, how their activities are perceived, how to promote better liaison and how they link with inner-city renewal policies being implemented by the local authority. The range of subjects discussed includes the promotion of a housing policy which ensures equal opportunity; a review of specific projects; the impact of local authority and government housing policies on local areas within the city; means of monitoring future activities of housing associations; employment practices within housing associations; and housing management practices with particular reference to local authority nominations and referrals.[9]

An example of what can be done by an individual association is provided by the Anchor Housing Association in Birmingham. Anchor has promised the allocation of all vacancies arising in areas with a high concentration of Asian and Afro-Caribbean people to Anil Bhalla who, as was noted on p. 48, maintains a list of older ethnic minority people in serious housing need. It is intended that this allocation should continue until the units concerned are all occupied by members of an ethnic minority, and that wardens from the appropriate ethnic groups should be appointed in due course. This policy has been justified, not on the basis of favouring a particular ethnic group, but because Anil Bhalla has been able to prove that by any standards the people on his waiting list are in more acute housing need than the elderly 'whites' who are also waiting for rehousing. Anchor has also appointed a full-time worker to specialise in provision for members of ethnic minorities in the Midlands region.

Local authority housing departments and ethnic minority groups
All this voluntary activity, important as it is, is of course minuscule in relation to overall need. The prime need for the elderly population in general is not for sheltered housing but for *appropriate* housing—in congenial surroundings and within reach of relevant community services. Basic systems of housing provision and allocation need to be reviewed if the particular needs of older people from the ethnic minority groups are to be adequately met. However, there is also a very serious need for local authorities to consider their policy in relation to sheltered housing. As we have seen in this chapter, social isolation, fear of harassment, language difficulties and inexperience in independent living make it important for older people from ethnic minorities, not only to be housed within their own communities, but also to be housed in groups so that they can provide mutual support and receive help from a warden or volunteer who is of the same ethnic background. So far, few housing authorities have provided any special treatment of this kind, with the result that hardly any sheltered housing is taken up by ethnic minority older people. As with housing associations, any special or grouped allocation needs to be done in very close association with the communities concerned and with support arrangements carefully worked out. Without this there is a real danger of putting

people into situations which only increase their isolation and fear and also of provoking a white backlash either by creating a focus for racist attack or by incurring hostility from white tenants. A great deal of care needs to be taken in developing mutual understanding and acceptance between established white tenants and ethnic minority newcomers. Hostility is largely a consequence of ignorance and fear, and if enough trouble is taken this can be overcome. The Anchor experiment in Birmingham may show ways in which mutual acceptance can be achieved.

Residential care

Very frail and disabled elderly members of ethnic minorities who need residential care present the greatest challenge to service providers. Their vulnerability and disability make their need for familiar, acceptable and comforting accommodation greater than at any other time in their lives, but providing this adequately is extremely difficult, especially as the overall numbers of any one ethnic group in any one place who need this type of care may be very small. The size of the Jewish community enables it to cope with this problem: the London Jewish Welfare Board runs fourteen homes, some with linked sheltered housing. There is also the huge Nightingale House in Lambeth with 395 beds. This is really several homes put together, each catering for different levels of need and ability. Its size means that it can offer a very full range of activities, plus dental, ophthalmological and chiropody services on the premises, and two doctors are in the building on five days a week. There is also associated sheltered housing.

The main European groups have also established specialist homes for their own older members, but the comparatively small numbers mean that residents have to come from a long distance and are therefore likely to be cut off from friends and family. In some cases, as in Slough (see p. 37), a local European community has got together to set up its own small residential care home. They hope to obtain a capital grant from joint funding money to convert a house and staff it with Polish nuns and volunteers.

The concept of residential care is often regarded with particular abhorrence by the Afro-Caribbeans and Asians; they see it as the epitome of what they regard as Western rejection of responsibility for the care of elderly relatives. Nevertheless, as we have seen from the demand for sheltered housing, by no means all the elderly people in these communities have families who are able and willing to look after them and, as those who are or who would like to be living independently get older and more frail, the need for intensive support will undoubtedly grow. To some extent it may be possible to meet this need by providing personal care in sheltered housing, but this will need to be purpose-built and designed for very disabled people. There is a strong case (as the working group quoted above has pointed out), for pilot projects in this field funded through a special allocation by the Housing Corporation and developed in close association with the local authority. One such scheme is already being developed by ASRA Leicester.

Another approach is to link sheltered housing with a local authority residential home and day care services, and build links between them so that the shock of transition, if it becomes necessary, is not too great. The potential for this exists in Frank Walsh House in Coventry, for instance, where a small residential care unit is attached to a day centre and a large sheltered housing complex in an area of high Asian population. Although the day centre is used by various groups of older Asian men on a self-run club basis, there are as yet only two Asian tenants in the sheltered housing and one Asian resident in the home. With care, skill and close co-operation, this whole complex could undoubtedly be used much more effectively to serve the Asian community than it is at present, but it does indicate the sort of development which might be acceptable. Something similar is planned in Sandwell where it is hoped to build links between an established residential home and a planned ASRA scheme close by. Further local authority sheltered housing for Asian use is also planned, including close association with a nearby Sikh temple, which is open all day and provides meals, entertainments and video shows. Really sensitive development of this kind can do a great deal to solve the problems, though we note again that it is easiest to cater for the language, diet and social customs of the largest groups and that those from smaller minorities may find that their particular needs are neglected.

Some experiments are being tried with setting aside beds in particular homes for particular groups. Bradford has selected two homes as residential and resource centres for older members of the Polish community and plans to employ some staff who speak Polish, possibly by splitting one current full-time care assistant post into two part-time posts and thus giving a spread of cover throughout the week. The danger here is that other European groups who have nothing in common with Polish people may be expected to accept and use the same service. Lambeth Social Services have also attempted to provide for elderly Afro-Caribbeans by offering facilities on a group basis in one of their homes, with suitable diet, recreational activities, and contact with appropriate community and religious organisations. Only two people have taken up the offer, however, perhaps because potential residents are reluctant to move away from their own community contacts in order to go into a home which may be some distance away.

Clearly there are no easy answers. Residential care is an emotive issue even for those who do not belong to an ethnic minority and providing it with the skill and sensitivity required to meet individual needs is not an easy task even where there are no cultural or linguistic difficulties. However, as *Home life: a code of practice for residential care homes*[10] reiterates again and again, it is by their success in achieving this that homes must be judged; local authorities now have a duty to see that homes in the private and voluntary sector provide care of this quality. It follows that local authorities also have a duty to see that their own homes do likewise. The more fully this goal is achieved for *all* residents, the better the particular needs of those from ethnic minorities will be met.

Conclusion
It will be obvious that there are no easy answers and no single answer to the housing needs of older members of ethnic minorities. At one end of the scale there is the political battle to be fought to eliminate racial discrimination in the allocation of housing and mortgages, and to ensure that housing associations and local authorities accept their responsibility to make appropriately placed and managed sheltered or grouped housing available to minority groups on an equitable basis. At the other extreme, there is the need for sensitive individual care and concern to ensure that housing goes to those who need it most, and that the right kind of support and help is offered in the right kind of way. It is a very considerable task and one which is only now beginning to be recognised. But ignoring it will not make it go away and the need for special provision can only become greater and more acute over at least the next twenty years.

SUMMARY OF ACTION REQUIRED

Action by ethnic minority groups
1. Put pressure on the local authority to operate an equitable policy of council housing allocation which takes account of the needs of

the ethnic minority communities in general and elderly people in particular.

2. Document and publicise the case for allocation of sheltered housing in appropriate locations and with appropriate warden support for elderly people from particular ethnic minority groups.

3. Recognise and exploit the potential of housing associations in providing sheltered housing designed, staffed and sited to suit the needs of particular ethnic minority groups.

Action by local authorities

1. Review and monitor employment and allocation policy in the housing department to eliminate racial discrimination.

2. Recognise the need for members of a particular ethnic group to be housed within reach of appropriate facilities, and in particular the need for older people to be in a familiar environment, able to communicate with neighbours, receive community support and be physically safe.

3. Consider provision of appropriate housing (sheltered or otherwise), managed in very close association with the community concerned.

4. Take care to ensure that ethnic minority groups are fully informed of their rights and opportunities when a Housing Action Area is declared.

5. Give urgent consideration to providing very sheltered housing or residential care in a form which is acceptable to very frail or disabled elderly members of ethnic minorities, and to means of building bridges between such services and specialist voluntary organisations.

Action by the Housing Corporation

1. Pursue a positive policy of encouraging the development of specialist sheltered housing and give particularly sympathetic consideration to the establishment of new housing associations by ethnic minority groups who want to work in this field.

2. Revise the rules governing grant allocation to allow the construction of houses and flats which are large enough to cater for extended families.

3. Set up experimental pilot projects with special funding to provide specialist very sheltered housing in close association with the local authority and particular ethnic minority groups.

Action by housing associations

1. Review and monitor policy of allocating existing stock in areas with a high concentration of particular ethnic minority groups.

2. Collaborate closely with appropriate ethnic minority organisations in the management of housing allocated to elderly people from an ethnic minority group.
3. Give sympathetic consideration to the use of resources to develop new projects in this field on behalf of relevant organisations using fair and fully-understood development and management agreements.
4. Review and monitor practices regarding employment, management and relationship to inner city renewal policies.

REFERENCES

1. Colin Brown, *Black and white in Britain, the third Policy Studies Institute survey*, Heinemann, London, 1984.
2. Atul Patel, *A description of the Asra Project in Highfields*, The Asra Project, Leicester Housing Association, 1982.
3. Anil Bhalla and Ken Blakemore, *Elders of the minority ethnic groups*, AFFOR, Birmingham, 1981.
4. Ros Lalljie, *Black elders: a discussion paper*, Research Section, Nottinghamshire County Council Social Services Department, Nottingham 1983.
5. See ref 2.
6. Age Concern England and Help the Aged Housing Trust, *Housing and related problems among elders in ethnic minorities: a working party report*, Age Concern, Mitcham, 1984.
7. National Federation of Housing Associations, *Race and housing: a guide for housing associations*, NFHA, London, 1982.
8. See ref 6.
9. Leeds Community Relations Council Housing Liaison Group, *Race and housing associations*, Leeds, 1984.
10. *Home Life: a code of practice for residential care*. Report of a Working Party sponsored by the DHSS and convened by the Centre for Policy on Ageing under the chairmanship of Kina, Lady Avebury. CPA, London, 1984.

4 Health needs and health services

Introduction

We know very little about use of the health service by members of ethnic minorities in any age group because there is a basic lack of such data on user activity, mortality and morbidity. This chapter attempts to pull together the even scantier information which is available in relation to older people and show how important it is to improve communication between service users and service providers and to open up access to services by going at least some way to meet the particular needs of ethnic minority patients. Maggie Pearson, director of the Centre for Ethnic Minorities Health Studies in Bradford, says of the National Health Service:

'... its policies and practices have understandably evolved in response to the needs of the white British population, as perceived by professionals and planners. This has entailed the development of culture-bound and 'colour-blind' policies which do not consider that established practice might be inappropriate for ethnic minority users, and are insensitive to their beliefs and way of life... Without a sensitive awareness of the assumptions on which the health services are based the ethnic minority user is easily defined as a problem person who needs special diets, female doctors, and interpreters, rather than attention being focused on the often inflexible and inappropriate nature of our institutions, professional practice and attitudes.

The overwhelming majority of health problems faced by ethnic minorities in Britain are different in degree, but not in kind from those experienced by the rest of the population. Social factors contributing to ill-health, and the general health care experience of the NHS are often intensified for the ethnic minority users by racism and racial prejudice, cultural insensitivity and language differences.'[1]

Institutionalised barriers to using the health service have been reinforced for many immigrants by their first bitter encounter with it when undergoing medical examinations on entering the country; and subsequently by the current hospital practice of demanding evidence of legal residence in the UK from people who 'look foreign'.

Health hazards for older immigrants

Fear of, and rejection by, the health service is doubly regrettable when one considers the degree of health risk incurred by elderly immigrants. The poor housing conditions which were described in the previous chapter give rise to health hazards from overcrowding and inadequate sanitation and heating. Men who cannot stay in their homes or lodgings during the day may be forced to wander in parks and shopping centres in all weathers and may try to blot out present reality and past trauma with alcohol. Women who are afraid to go out or unaccustomed to doing so may get too little exercise and sunshine as well as becoming socially isolated and depressed. Inadequate income may result in poor diet and insufficient warm clothing. A lifetime of work in dangerous or unhealthy conditions—on building sites, in steamy kitchens, in rag-trade sweatshops and in the least protected and hardest labouring jobs in industry—can create chronic illness and disability. In addition, for the present immigrant generation, there is the stress arising from facing old age 'in a strange land', homesickness for the country of origin, and, for those who are 'black' the constant tension of living with racial harassment and discrimination.

There may also be special health hazards for particular ethnic minority groups. Some inherited blood disorders are endemic in the Afro-Caribbean and Cypriot communities, while a high incidence of anaemia among Asian women is attributable to a diet which is short of vitamin D and not compensated for in this country by sunshine. Vitamin D deficiency can also cause osteomalacia—a form of old-age rickets—where there is severe pain in the joints, loss of mobility and a tendency to fractures. (This lack of vitamin D could be compensated for by adding it to chapatti flour at the manufacturing stage, but the DHSS working party on the subject did not think the situation sufficiently serious to warrant this.) As well as present dietary deficiencies, past lack of calcium and magnesium in the diet in the country of origin may result in the bones of immigrants becoming brittle in middle age. There is also evidence, summarised by Allan McNaught in his paper *Race and health care in the United Kingdom*[2] that immigrants from the Caribbean and Africa suffer particularly from diabetes, hypertension and strokes though they have relatively little heart disease.

Contact with general practitioners
A large-scale household survey in inner areas of the West Midlands conurbation carried out in 1981 found that over 99 per cent of 'all groups', (white, Asian and Afro-Caribbean) were registered with a GP, and only about ten per cent were not registered with a GP practising in their immediate area of residence. Sixty-six per cent of all

Asians had a GP of Asian origin and a further ten per cent were registered with practices containing an Asian doctor (though it cannot of course be assumed that he spoke the same language as his patient).[3]

Although Asians may find it relatively easy to find a GP who can speak their language, elderly people from smaller or more scattered communities may find it extremely difficult to do so. The Chinese and Cypriot communities report particular difficulties in this regard—and of course the same applies with equal force to other health services.

An analysis by Blakemore of data from the AFFOR survey[4] found, as the table below shows, that a high proportion of elderly Asians and Afro-Caribbeans had visited their general practitioner within the previous year. In this respect there was a statistically significant difference from the Europeans in the sample, though the European group were older and might therefore have been expected to have a higher proportion of consultations.

Table 6.   Visits to a general practitioner by ethnic group (percentages)

When visited	Afro-Caribbeans	Asians	Europeans
	%	%	%
Within last month*	68	70	53
Within last 12 months*	23	22	23
Long/Don't know	9	8	24
Total	100	100	100
Number	179	169	52

*from date of interview.

Source: Kenneth Blakemore 'Health and Illness among the elderly of minority ethnic groups living in Birmingham: some new findings', in *Health Trends*, Vol. 14, no 3, p. 70, 1982.

Another study of mainly younger people carried out by the Research Unit for Ethnic Relations at the University of Aston[5] confirms this finding. Twenty-seven per cent of white respondents had *not* visited a GP in the 12 months before the interview compared with 18 per cent of Afro-Caribbeans and eight per cent of Asians.

However, it is one thing to go to the doctor and appreciate the service offered and quite another to get effective help. There was widespread agreement among informants that a sense of pressure in doctors' surgeries and difficulties in communication often made consultations less than satisfactory, even when there was no obvious language barrier. Such problems with communication, which are also frequently found in contacts between GPs and indigenous elderly people, arise from the use of medical jargon without proper explanation, the difficulty for a patient of describing pain and illness in medical terms, a wide culture gap between doctor and patient (even if they are from the same community), reluctance to undergo a physical examination, and simple shyness. Some patients, and especially those from a very rural background, may also have a deeply-held and perhaps justified conviction that the less people in authority know about you, the less harm they can do you. Philip Rack in his book *Race, culture and mental disorder*[6] suggests that when dealing with people from a rural culture

'the doctor or social worker who tries conscientiously to obtain a detailed social history, and attempts to record the names, ages, and other details of every member of the family is pretty certain to meet a blank look. The patient has forgotten or suddenly ceases to understand English. Polite small-talk with enquiries about absent relatives or conditions back home may be regarded as snooping. Anyone whose role is not clearly defined and recognised—such as a health visitor or school liaison officer— may be a spy for the police, or Home Office immigration department, or 'them'. Even the doctor, whose role is accepted, arouses suspicion if he takes too much interest in illnesses of the past, which in the patient's view have no relevance to the present.'

Even if good communication with the GP is established and the appropriate medicine is obtained it may not be taken correctly. Mays and Donaldson[7] quote a Birmingham study which found that illiteracy and poor comprehension of English, in addition to unfamiliarity with Western medicine, led to misuse of medication among Asian patients. The situation was greatly improved by personal counselling of patients in their own first language by a skilled pharmacist, accompanied by full instruction leaflets. These leaflets were mainly for relatives to read, and were in English because most people who were fully literate in their own language could also read English.

These difficulties in communication, together with crowded surgeries and lack of confidence in the GP's knowledge of tropical diseases like sickle-cell anaemia and yaws, often encourage people of Afro-Caribbean origin to pay privately for a second opinion or for 'better treatment'. The Nottinghamshire survey quotes Weightman[8] as suggesting that this is because there is more informality in the doctor-patient relationship in the West Indies compared with the brevity and formality of contacts with NHS doctors who are felt to provide only a cursory appraisal of the patient's problems. Over half the respondents in the Nottinghamshire survey had consulted a private GP whilst they had lived in this country, 20 within the last twelve months; 42 said it was to get a second opinion, sixteen to get a better examination and sixteen gave other reasons.[9]

Asians, however, do not appear to consult private GPs more often than Europeans, and the Johnson and Cross study found that in the West Midlands they did not make much use of traditional holistic medicine practised by Unani or Ayurvedic 'Hakims' either. However, an article in *Geriatric Medicine*[10] reports a study undertaken by Davies and Aslam for the DHSS which found that:

... 'Hakims or traditional healers from the Indian sub-continent are at work in all the main Asian communities in Britain. Patients are often found to be employing a dual approach to treatment, consulting both Hakim and GP for the same condition'.

The article continues:

'In the Indian sub-continent, two traditional systems of medicine operate side by side with Western medicine: the Unani system, and the Ayurvedic system. Both systems consider the importance of temperament, the balance of humours, diet and lifestyle, in the causation and appropriate treatment of ailments. Hakims are registered by the government of India and Pakistan, and train for four to five years at schools for traditional medicine. They thus represent a true alternative to Western medicine and are not the fringe operators that some in the West might believe them to be. However, in Britain there is, as yet, no system of registration, and qualified and unqualified Hakims are at work.

Some patients go to Hakims because they feel let down by Western medicine, and some go because they have always gone to a Hakim, among whom the elderly are likely to predominate.

Hakims do seem to provide a successful and valuable service which people continue to want even with the greatly increased availability of conventional Western medicine in Britain. It would appear that patients have more confidence in traditional healers and appreciate the holistic approach taken to symptomatology and diagnosis.

What is most crucial is the fact that Western-trained doctors including in many cases Asians, seem largely unaware of the work of the Hakims. A very real danger is that they may overlook the possibility that some of the symptoms they see could be the result of the interaction between their drugs and those prescribed by the Hakim. In an elderly person who is more likely than most to be receiving multiple medication from a Western GP, the side-effects could be extremely harmful.'

Contact with community-based health services
The role of the GP is at least well accepted and well understood. That of other community-based NHS staff may be much less so. Community nurses in particular seem to have almost no contact with older people from ethnic minorities. Six community nurses in a modern health centre on the edge of Chapeltown in Leeds talked with passion to the author of this report about the early discharge from hospital and the shortage of home help and residential places which they felt were putting their elderly European clients at severe risk, but they had very few West Indian or Asian clients of any age, and these were straightforward treatment cases. Yet, as has already been demonstrated, the need of older members of ethnic minorities for greater understanding of their health problems and of services to meet them remains acute. There seems to be a very strong case for offering more advice sessions on the health visitor model and talks on general health education in the specialist clubs, day centres, temples and churches where ethnic minority elders may be found. It is clear that when this is done it is very popular. There must be many qualified nurses with the appropriate ethnic background and language skills who with suitable training could provide such an educational service on a peripatetic basis.

Access to hospital services
The AFFOR data shows a high use of hospital services amongst Afro-Caribbean elders, while hospital use among Asians is less than would be expected from the health risks to which they are subject.

Table 7. Visits to hospital by ethnic group (percentages)

Visits in previous 12 months*	Afro-Caribbeans	Asians	Europeans
	%	%	%
Once	23	18	17
Twice or more	19	7	12
Never	58	75	71
Total	100	100	100
Number	179	169	52

*from date of interview.

Source: Kenneth Blakemore 'Health and Illness among the elderly of minority ethnic groups living in Birmingham: some new findings', in *Health Trends* Vol. 14, no 3, 1982.

Blakemore comments:

'Over two-fifths of the Afro-Caribbean elderly had been to hospital and in this respect they stand out as a group with a particularly high level of health problems; the difference between them, and the Asian and European elderly is statistically significant ($P = 0.0001$). It is the high proportion of Afro-Caribbean women—almost half—who had visited hospital which accounts for this ethnic difference; the proportion of Afro-Caribbean men who had visited hospital, though somewhat higher than that of European and Asian men, is not significantly different.'

Relatively low use of hospital services by the Asian groups probably reflects the special difficulties which many Asians have in using the service as it is provided at present. Hospitals are frightening and confusing places for elderly people from any background; much more so if the staff cannot understand what you are saying and cannot make themselves understood, if you cannot eat the food, and your body is exposed and handled in a way which you find shaming and distressing. A member of Southall Scope surveying the health problems of older Asians observed 'many people I spoke to were not prepared to go to hospital, partly because of the food they would be given, but also as a result of reports from friends or acquaintances of bad treatment within the hospital service'.[11] (The whole issue of specialist food is discussed more fully in the next chapter.) There are no simple solutions but a checklist on *Providing effective health care in a multi-racial society,*[12] suggests the following measures in hospital and community health services:

'Signs and directions around the hospital in community languages.

Appropriate food and catering arrangements that take into account patients' religious dietary rules, the normal diet of the communities from which they come, patients' wishes to fast, etc.

Practical provision on the wards for patients' preferences in personal hygiene, e.g., washing with water after using the lavatory, showering rather than sitting in a bath, rubbing their hair with oil, or washing before any food or drink is taken.

Visiting arrangements geared to variations in family responsibility and obligations among patients' relatives. In hospitals where there are large numbers of visitors due to a high proportion of patients having extended families, open visiting may be a more appropriate system. Restricting visiting may be distressing and offensive to some communities. For example, in some Jewish families the moral obligation to visit is as strong as the obligation to pray for the patient, as visiting represents an act of charity which mitigates the patient's suffering.

Interpreters provided to interpret for patients, doctors, nurses and other staff whenever necessary.

Interpreters or bilingual staff visiting new patients to explain hospital routines and provision, and to sort out any problems or worries.

Training for staff to ensure a generally positive and well-informed attitude towards minority group patients' individual needs and wishes.

Diet leaflets appropriate to the habits of different minority groups and referring to foods that are part of their normal diet.

Leaflets translated into the main community languages and/or in plain English.

Training for dietitians and catering managers about the dietary habits and norms of different minority communities.

Active recruitment of dietitians and catering staff who speak the languages and share the culture and backgrounds of local minority groups.

Provision of appropriate and acceptable food in hospitals.

Training receptionists, medical records staff, and ward clerks in how to record names, how to avoid entering mistakes in records, and how to sort out existing confusion.

Training for nursing staff in the different naming systems and how to address people correctly and politely'.

The action needed from the DHSS and the health authorities to achieve good practice is summarised below (pp. 69–71).

Psychiatric illness and treatment

Physical illness and disability in a foreign land is painful and frightening enough; to suffer mental illness is doubly so. As CPA has described at length in another report,[13] old age is a time of mental as well as physical vulnerability. Physical illnesses of many kinds can produce an acute state of confusion; depressive illness and severe anxiety are common; some older people develop fixed delusional symptoms of persecution. All these conditions can be treated, usually with success if they are correctly diagnosed and skilled help is available. A small percentage of older people, especially those in their eighties and nineties, are also vulnerable to dementia—that is, organic illness which causes progressive mental impairment and loss of short-term memory through failure of blood supply to the brain cells (multi-infarct dementia) or through a complex syndrome of disease processes relating to the chemistry of the brain (dementia of the Alzheimer type). Vulnerability to any of these illnesses is common amongst older people of any background but those from immigrant ethnic groups are particularly at risk. As we have seen, these elders have often suffered from a deep and multi-faceted loss—loss of their homeland, of social role and status, of a familiar and safe environment, of easy verbal communication, sometimes even with young members of their own family. It would be surprising if depression and anxiety were not common amongst them and reports from all the communities concerned indicate that this is the case. Past persecution and maltreatment and forgetting learned languages in old age also enhance the risk of paranoid feelings and may generate a vicious circle of fear and hostility. Those suffering from dementia are most vulnerable of all. Because severe loss of short-term memory is the primary symptom they may be utterly bewildered by the surroundings in which they find themselves, not remembering where they are and how they got there and this must be a very frightening experience indeed. It seems likely that dementia, especially of the Alzheimer type, is still uncommon in most of the ethnic minorities since the older generation are still relatively young and its incidence increases greatly with age, but it is certainly something that the Jewish voluntary services and those dealing with elderly Europeans are having to contend with, and it is likely to become a major challenge for all the communities in the years ahead unless a way of preventing or curing the illness can be found.

The provision of psychogeriatric services for indigenous elderly people is still relatively new and very uneven in quality and resource allocation. Providing adequately for settlers seems likely to be an even harder task, partly because there may be great reluctance to refer people who need help, partly because it may be very difficult for observers to distinguish cultural characteristics from symptoms of illness (this is certainly true in relation to schizophrenia in younger age groups), and partly because the language and cultural barriers compound the difficulty of offering understanding and treatment. There are no simple or easy answers but it is clearly essential that general practitioners, community leaders and care givers should be informed about these conditions and know where to seek help and advice if someone's behaviour is giving cause for concern. It is a tragedy if symptoms which produce unacceptable behaviour or which necessitate hospital admission should result in the ill person's rejection by their family and community; it is equally tragic if no help or treatment is offered and the sufferer is hidden and the symptoms hushed up. Mental illness is no greater a disgrace than physical illness and we must learn how to offer acceptable treatment and help to sufferers of any age and ethnic background.

DHSS responsibility
Clearly an immense amount needs to be done, and it is unlikely that the regional and district health authorities will take the need and the urgency seriously enough unless they are given a clear lead from the top. The DHSS needs to develop a strategy and demonstrate greater leadership and commitment in this field. McNaught[14] makes the following suggestions for DHSS action:

1. The development of a clear *policy statement* which sets out in broad terms the approach the DHSS expects health authorities

to bear in mind in providing services to multi-racial populations. This statement would also provide a framework for health policy activities in the DHSS itself.

2. A small number of health authorities should be used as 'test tubes' to monitor the development of race relations policy. From this process good practice or models could be developed and used to improve practices on a wider scale.

3. The financing or promotion of *demonstration projects,* which are focused on action, rather than education.

4. Using *Annual Review Meetings* to encourage and monitor the development of race relations policy in health authorities.

5. Extend the work of Branch 3 (the Health Service Division assigned the responsibility for the race/ethnic dimension of the DHSS's work) to include consideration of manpower, training and planning: either by attaching staff from those divisions, or through the development of some co-ordinating mechanism between the branches or divisions concerned.

District Health Authority (DHA) responsibility
A lead from the DHSS needs to be complemented by real commitment at health district level. McNaught sums up the sort of management action needed in the following terms:

'The development of a race relations policy requires DHA members, District and Unit Management Teams, individual managers and professional staff to demonstrate leadership and commitment to racial equality. In local authorities commitment has been signalled by the appointment of race relations advisers, the establishment of specialist units and committees to monitor the functioning of the authority, provide advice to management and to oversee the implementation of the authority's strategy. Few signs of a similar commitment and action have been forthcoming from the national health service, ... while the dominant framework in the national health service for looking at black and ethnic minorities is to see them as a burden on well-functioning services, rather than a section of the population whose needs automatically merit consideration, without elaborate justification.'

He makes the following recommendations:

1. The establishment of a small members' working group to maintain a watching brief on ethnic minority health and related issues in the Authority.

2. The designation of a senior officer on the staff of the authority's administrator as being responsible for monitoring this issue in the day-to-day work of the authority and for the implementation of the authority's strategy.

3. The establishment of a small multi-disciplinary advisory group of senior officers and professionals to formulate a strategy and detailed advice for the authority's management.

It is noteworthy that Haringey health authority has secured the support of the King's Fund for the three-year appointment of an adviser in the field of ethnic relations to help the district develop an action programme. It is hoped that at the end of the period a significant shift will have occurred in the awareness and understanding of authority and management team members, managers and staff. 'Managers will be in a position to develop services in response to racial influence in the same way as they currently respond to influences of age, sex, morbidity and resources'. The post will, it is hoped, pump-prime these processes to the point where they begin to be integrated into the fabric of management in the district.[15]

Community Health Council (CHC) responsibility
Pressure for reform also needs to come from below. The community health councils should be doing much more than they are at present to fulfil their role as consumer representatives in the national health service; they need to make sure that black and ethnic minority organisations are on the list of bodies from which CHC members are selected. CHCs and other concerned pressure groups now have a useful tool in the form of the recently published checklist on providing health care in a multi-racial society referred to above.[16] This deals with different aspects of health care through questions, information and recommendations about good practice and provides a starting point for consideration of local research, training needs, improvement of individual professional practice and review of service delivery.

Community health initiatives
Another important starting point is in community health work, and funding should be made available for posts such as that recently set

up by the Asian Community Action Group in Lambeth. The most immediate tasks of the worker are to:

1. act as a source of information and advice on health matters and rights to enable the Asian community to make better use of health services available.

2. facilitate the formation of groups within the Asian community which can promote discussion and mutual support with regard to their health care and confidence to demand a better health service.

3. work with other groups to press systematically for positive changes in the health service provided by the health authorities in Lambeth.

Specialist workers of this kind are urgently needed in all the main concentrations of ethnic minorities, but they are few and far between at present.

Another innovation, also in Lambeth, was the appointment of a community health worker for ethnic minorities sponsored jointly by Community Service Volunteers and the project team for a new health centre. The objective of this post was to build a profile of the health needs of the various community groups, involve local people in their own health issues and ensure that their needs are met. The centre itself is an ambitious project. It is hoped to offer therapies which include dentistry, chiropody, audiometry, physiotherapy, occupational therapy and diversional activities and the centre will also seek to treat withdrawal and loss of social skills by accepting up to 30 people daily for group rehabilitation. Individual help will include bereavement counselling and advice on welfare benefits as well as physical treatments.

The project team are anxious that the Asian and Afro-Caribbean communities should be able to make full use of the facilities. Efforts are being made to cater for special needs in terms of food, language, library facilities and provision of a quiet area for prayer, and one of the GPs giving a weekly session will be Asian.

Another community-based innovation is the Asian Stroke Club in Birmingham which is funded by the Social Services Department. This club was set up because the hospitals were concerned about the lack of facilities to meet the needs of the large number of

middle-aged Asian men suffering from strokes who needed rehabilitation . It offers a range of therapies, including speech therapy and
swimming, in a way which is acceptable in linguistic and cultural
terms, and it is hoped to minimise transport problems by taking the
club to different parts of the city on different days of the week. Anil
Bhalla (see p. 47) is one of the workers involved in this project and
he hopes to make the club one part of a range of services financed by
mainstream funding and including day centre and holiday provision
as well as the development of sheltered housing.

Another possible way forward is the appointment of specialists to
work with older people in the minority groups suffering from particular disabilities. Thus, Leicestershire social services department's
review of services to the elderly points up the need for a senior
occupational therapist to work with elderly ethnic minority people
and their families and the need to create capacity for appropriate
specialists to work with those suffering from visual and aural handicap.[17] Where numbers justify it, the communities themselves may
make special provision. The Jewish Blind Society, for example,
employs a specialist worker who visits individuals in the whole of
South East England and who runs a weekly Jewish Blind Club in
Brixton which draws members from a wide catchment area.

Training and research initiatives
Better training for all the professions involved in health service provision is obviously a basic necessity and it is encouraging that the
Junior Members Forum of the British Medical Association recently
discussed this matter and agreed that:

1. the board of science and education should examine and report
   on the action needed to meet the health needs of ethnic
   minorities.

2. the BMA council should (a) approach the relevant education
   authorities with a view to introducing an appropriate medical
   undergraduate curriculum to improve awareness of the effect
   of racial and cultural differences on the delivery of health care
   to ethnic minorities; (b) establish links at local, regional and
   national levels between the profession and organisations
   representing the health needs of the ethnic minority groups;
   (c) explore ways to make health care more acceptable to ethnic
   minorities; (d) explore ways to educate ethnic minority groups
   to make better use of existing provisions.

3. the recruitment of health care professionals fluent in the language of the ethnic minorities should be encouraged.[18]

One project, 'Training in health and race', has already been launched by the National Extension College with backing from the Health Education Council, to provide training and resources for health professionals in this field. It published the checklist referred to above, (pp 66–68) and has a co-ordinator based in London with regional research and development officers in Birmingham, Leeds, Leicester and London. Another important initiative is the Centre for Ethnic Minorities' Health Studies at Bradford. This is a national multi-disciplinary research, resource and educational centre for the study of health care needs of ethnic minorities in Britain whose aims are:

1. To bring together in one place information about the health care problems of ethnic minorities in Britain and make this information available to those who need it.

2. To act as a resource and reference centre for practitioners and researchers working in this field, so that research findings may be made known promptly and a directory of expertise and good practice made available.

3. To organise training and education courses, seminars and conferences on relevant issues, independently or in association with other educational bodies and health authorities.

4. To initiate new research on specific subjects by obtaining research grants from national and international sources and provide academic and practical backing for new or existing projects.

Another initiative is the Community Health Group for Ethnic Minorities. This sets out to act as a forum for discussion and study of health and social services provision and to offer a multi-lingual interpreting and translating service for professionals working in the field which it calls 'The Ethnic Switchboard'.

As a final example of the new developments, contact is at last beginning to grow between representatives of the ethnic minorities and the Institution of Environmental Health Officers. This is long overdue, since environmental health work brings, or should bring, officers into frequent contact with minority groups through their responsibility for enforcement of the Housing Acts and legislation governing food hygiene, promotion of health and safety in commercial and industrial premises, and encouragement of home safety. A working party has now been set up by the Institution and the Commission for Racial Equality (CRE) to prepare a policy document which should provide the foundation for much further work.[19]

All these initiatives (and there are no doubt many others) are encouraging, but they are just the beginning of the immensely challenging and urgent task of making all health services available to all the residents of the United Kingdom on equal terms.

Conclusion
This chapter has outlined what can be seen as the inhospitality of hospital and other health services to members of ethnic minority groups, and especially to elderly people, many of whom are at serious risk. They do desperately need the service, but they cannot use it as it is at present provided. Changes are needed at all levels of service provision—changes in attitude towards consumer need, in employment policy, in administrative practice and in where and how services are offered. As in so many areas discussed in this report, the particular needs of ethnic minority groups have highlighted shortcomings in service provision and practice which affect the whole population. Decentralised peripatetic treatment facilities, GPs who care about communication with their patients, comprehensible instructions on medication, properly sign-posted hospital corridors, edible hospital food, flexible visiting hours, the opportunity to ask questions and receive information—these are not peculiar or unusual needs. They are common to all users of the national health service, and as much attention should be given to them as to other aspects of professional practice. It is no good providing a superb clinical service if people cannot use it, or if they are confused, frightened and unhappy when they try to do so. There is much which can be done without enormous expense to improve the mode of service provision, if only we have the will to do so. For the present generation of elderly settlers, such improvement is desperately urgent. If we do not achieve it they are condemned to years of unnecessary pain and illness, and perhaps to death, for the crime of coming from another culture.

SUMMARY OF ACTION REQUIRED

Action by ethnic minority groups

1. Make use of religious and community centres, clubs and day centres as a base for health education (including mental health) and press for treatment facilities to be provided on a local basis.
2. Press for representation of ethnic minorities on community health councils and encourage CHCs to campaign for improved services for these groups on the lines recommended in the checklist.
3. Campaign through the national political parties for action on specific issues, such as the inclusion of Vitamin D in chapatti flour.
4. Work with hospitals, health centres and family practitioner committees to encourage the appointment, training and deployment of 'link people' with suitable ethnic background and language skills to act as interpreters and intermediaries.
5. Seek funding for the appointment of community health workers to work with a particular day centre or action group to mobilise services and pinpoint needs.
6. Keep in touch with, and publicise the findings of, projects such as the Centre for Ethnic Minorities' Health Studies.

Action by general practitioners

1. Take trouble to find out about the cultural characteristics, attitudes to health and illness, possible health hazards, and proper nomenclature of the ethnic groups in the practice.
2. Ensure that practice nurses, receptionists and other staff have similar knowledge and, if possible, a range of linguistic skills. Make arrangements to obtain interpreter services when required. Take particular care to make sure that explanations and instructions are understood.
3. Establish a close working relationship with pharmacists of appropriate ethnic backgrounds.

Action by health authorities

1. Demonstrate a real commitment to providing equality of opportunity within the service; review and monitor processes of recruitment, training, staff deployment and staff promotion to make this a reality.
2. Define a programme of action based on the checklist and monitor progress in association with the communities concerned.
3. Work with broadly-based CHCs and the ethnic minority com-

munities concerned to identify local needs for service provision and barriers in using the present service.

4. Explore means of deploying nurses, doctors, physiotherapists, etc. who are normally hospital-based on a sessional basis in accessible community premises and supply associated interpreter facilities. (One model for such deployment can be found in Portsmouth's peripatetic psychogeriatric unit.)
5. Ensure that new health centres and other facilities take full account of the needs of ethnic minorities in design, facilities and mode of service provision.
6. Recruit and deploy personnel who can provide health education and preventive services in established community groups.
7. To promote these and other policies, each health authority should carry out the suggestions listed on p 71, that is:

   i) Establish a small members' working group to maintain a watching brief on ethnic minority health and related issues in the authority.
   ii) Designate a senior officer on the staff of the authority's administration as being responsible for monitoring this issue in the day-to-day work of the authority and for the implementation of the authority's strategy.
   iii) Establish a small multi-disciplinary advisory group of senior officers and professionals to formulate a strategy and detailed advice for the authority's management.

Action by central government

1. Make section 11 funding (see p 140) available to the health service as well as to local authorities, and encourage its use to develop interpreter services and the employment of staff to meet the needs of particular ethnic minority groups.
2. Carry out the actions suggested on p 69:
   i) Develop a clear policy statement which sets out in broad terms the approach the DHSS expects health authorities to bear in mind in providing services to multi-racial populations.
   ii) Use a small number of health authorities to monitor the development of race relations policy and develop models which could be used to improve practices on a wider scale.
   iii) Finance or promote demonstration projects, which are focussed on action rather than education.
   iv) Use Annual Review Meetings to encourage and monitor the development of race relations policy in health authorities.

v) Extend the work of Branch 3 (the Health Service Division with responsibility for race/ethnic dimension of the DHSS's work) to include consideration of manpower, training and planning.

REFERENCES

1. Maggie Pearson, An insensitive service, in Anthony Harrison and John Gretton (eds), *Health Care UK 1984: an economic, social and policy audit.* Chartered Institute of Public Finance and Accountancy, London, 1984, p. 122.
2. Allan McNaught, *Race and health care in the United Kingdom,* Occasional papers in health service administration, Centre for Health Service Management Studies, Polytechnic of the South Bank, London, 1984.
3. M R D Johnson and M Cross, How ethnic minorities use health services, *CHC News,* January/February 1983, p 6.
4. Ken Blakemore, Health and illness among the elderly of minority ethnic groups living in Birmingham: some new findings, *Health Trends,* vol. 14, no 3, 1982, pp 69–72.
5. Ibid, quoting M Johnson, M Cross and R Parker, unpublished conference paper, Institute of British Geographers, 1982.
6. Philip Rack, *Race, culture and mental disorder,* Tavistock Publications, London, 1982.
7. Nicholas B Mays and L J Donaldson, *Feasibility study of the health and social needs of elderly Asians,* Leicester Inner Area Programme, Department of Community Health, Leicester Royal Infirmary, 1981.
8. Gavin Weightman, Poor man's Harley Street, *New Society* 20 October 1977, pp 118–9.
9. Stewart Berry, Mike Lee, Sue Griffiths, *Report on a survey of West Indian pensioners in Nottingham,* Nottinghamshire County Council Social Services Department Research section, January 1981.
10. Nicholas Mays, The health needs of elderly Asians, *Geriatric Medicine,* vol. 11, no 11, November 1981 p 41.
11. Haringey Community Relations Council, *The ethnic elderly: Asians, Cypriots, West Indians.* Haringey CRC, London, 1979.
12. Health Education Council and National Extension College for Training in Health and Race, *Providing effective health care in a multi-racial society: a checklist for looking at local issues,* HEC and NEC, London, 1984.
13. Alison Norman, *Mental illness in old age: meeting the challenge,* Centre for Policy on Ageing, London, 1982.
14. See ref 2.
15. Paul Mitchell, Multiculture care, *Health and Social Service Journal,* 30 August 1984, pp 1032–3.
16. See ref 12.
17. Leicestershire County Council Social Services Department, *Services for the elderly.* LCC, 1983.
18. Linda Beecham, Health problems of ethnic minorities, *British Medical Journal,* vol. 286, 9 April 1983 p 1226–7.
19. A special correspondent, Improving communications with ethnic minorities. *Municipal Journal,* 18 February 1983, p 219.

5 Voluntary day centre provision

Introduction

The first chapters of this report have described the extent to which the immigrant generation of people who have grown up in another culture and are now growing old in the United Kingdom may be socially isolated, suffering from loss of traditional roles, out of touch with their previous homeland and culture, living in poor housing conditions and without adequate health care. They are also unable to make use of the immense range of clubs and day centres now available to indigenous pensioners in most urban areas. This is because they feel unwelcomed by the membership; the food served may be either unpalatable or inedible because of dietary custom or religious belief; the activities on offer may not be interesting or relevant to them; mixing of the sexes may be unacceptable; and there may be major language barriers. These negative reasons for needing clubs and day centres which cater for particular ethnic groups are, however, of less importance than the positive desire to have a place in which to relax, meet friends, make a contribution to the well-being of others, exercise existing skills and learn new ones, and to read papers and books and watch video films related to one's own culture and country of origin.

Awareness of the need for specialist day centres and clubs has crystallised during the early 1980s and an immense amount has been done to meet the need through voluntary initiatives within the communities concerned. Over forty examples of such voluntary centres were visited in the course of preparing this report, and Appendix 1 gives brief details of each so that readers can identify and make contact with those which they would like to know more about. They include Asian, Afro-Caribbean, Cypriot and Jewish initiatives, but the author was also told of schemes emerging to meet the needs of Polish, Chinese and Irish people, and it is clear that a demand for specialist provision of this kind is common to all ethnic minority groups. Such centres do far more than provide a focus of social activity. They are a basis for advice-giving, language teaching, health education and outreach support of people in their own homes, and also a means of articulating the needs of their members in relation to established services. They are therefore a key to effective provision of services for elderly immigrants, and their support by and relationship to local authorities is of basic importance. This chapter attempts to summarise their characteristics in general terms and to bring out issues relevant to initiators, local authorities and funding bodies. The selection of centres to visit was largely determined by availability of information about their existence, ability to make contact, and geographical location. The time schedule was very tight so that, although an attempt was made to cover a wide range in terms of ethnic group, size, objectives and management style, there has been no attempt at comprehensive coverage. It is hoped, however, that enough ground has been covered to indicate the immense potential of developments of this kind.

Asian day centres and clubs

Asian day centres differ from those of other ethnic groups in that the main group for which they cater at present comprises men in their fifties and sixties who are unemployed and often without anywhere to go during the day. This is because it is not culturally acceptable for them to stay at home with unchaperoned female relatives or because there is no room at home for them to invite friends in to talk or play cards. Although they may be relatively young, these men are often, as has already been noted, in poor physical health as a result of previous hardships and present low income and overcrowded housing. Most centres cater for a mix of Hindus and Sikhs, and meals, if they are served, are vegetarian. Moslems generally have separate provision and this is at present much less developed. When women are catered for, it is usually by allowing them use of a room or rooms on particular days or, as in Scope Ealing (no 1)* by setting aside a floor for their exclusive use. In some of the Midland cities where users are mainly Gujarati immigrants from East Africa, men and women are catered for together (nos 9, 10, 11). Facilities provided for women tend to be focussed on particular activities such as language classes, dressmaking, traditional crafts, health education or religious practices, while provision for men usually includes card games and a range of papers and magazines from the country of origin. Video films are very popular when the equipment is available. Though there is a general 'family likeness' these clubs and centres vary greatly in size, staffing, funding, quality of premises and the range of facilities which they can offer. At one end of the scale, there are large, well-established centres in reasonably suitable premises open at least five days a week and providing a wide range of facilities such as Scope Ealing (no 1), Milap Ealing (no 2), Brent Asian Elders (no 5) and Scope Leicester (no 9). At the other end of the scale, there are small self-help groups like the Stonebridge Asian Elders Social Group which meets in cramped conditions in a community centre (no 6) and the pensioners group using the Asian Centre in Haringey (no 3).

*The numbers refer to clubs and day centres described in Appendix 1, pp 150–170.

In some cases, facilities are provided by another organisation which may be either religious or secular; for example, the centres run under the auspices of the Indian Workers Association (no 12) and Guru Nanak Temple in Bradford (no 13), the Indian Community Centre in Nottingham (no 11) and the very ambitious project planned at the Central Mosque in Birmingham (no 15).

When clubs cannot obtain any permanent home, they often meet for a day or half a day in some borrowed room. Thus, the Asian Women's Group in Haringey (no 4) is not allowed to use the Asian Centre, because their main activity is religious. (Religious practices are not allowed at the Centre because it is feared that they would dominate its use and exacerbate conflict between members of different faiths.) The women have to use the corner of a huge, draughty church hall where they put up a portable shrine which closes up like a triptych and spread a rug so that the corner becomes a little temple.

Although there are notable exceptions, standards of decoration and comfort often leave a good deal to be desired because of lack of funding or the need to use shared premises. The worst example found of over-crowding, poor furnishing and decoration and lack of facilities, is the centre run by Wolverhampton Community Relations Council (CRC) in two small rooms at the back of their own premises (no 16). This is not the fault of the CRC which has done its utmost to obtain funding for more adequate provision, and it says much for the desperation of older Asian men who have nowhere to go during the day that they are prepared to use the centre. The local authority did put up £1,000 to provide a video and TV set, but refused more on the grounds that the premises were so poor that they could not justify putting more resources into them.

Afro-Caribbean day centres and clubs
As with initiatives arising from the Asian communities, the Afro-Caribbean centres have a strong basic similarity, though there are wide differences in size, range of services and staff levels. They have very often been set up as a result of the energetic efforts of an individual—but sometimes by a church or a community association. Membership is predominantly female—perhaps about 75 per cent on average; lunch is usually cooked on the premises; there is a strong emphasis on craft activities, using traditional skills and achieving work of a very high standard which is sold for fund-raising; and some traditional games, such as dominoes, are popular. Advice-giving is usually on an informal basis, though seen as a very

important aspect of service, and there is a strong tendency to develop outreach work in terms of delivering meals to members who cannot get to the centre, providing personal care and support for housebound people and visiting people in hospital. With the exception of the West Indian Senior Citizens Club in Brixton (no 21), all the projects visited were run in premises belonging to another organisation. Some were in church halls, some in community centres (but never new, purpose-built ones) and some in buildings belonging to the parent organisation. Premises are far from ideal and suffer from lack of accessibility for disabled people, inadequate toilet facilities, lack of storage space and competition with other groups using the building. The longing to have a 'place of our own' was widespread and in two cases—the Pepper Pot Club in North Kensington (no 24) and the Welcome Club in Brent (no 18), this was about to be achieved at the time of the visit. The only centre operating in newly-converted and very well equipped premises—the Brixton West Indian Senior Citizens Club (no 21)—obtained them after a very lengthy struggle to convince the funding authorities of the need and then only when their previous accommodation had literally collapsed around them. The warmth and friendliness of the atmosphere in these Afro-Caribbean clubs was very noticeable and they clearly have a lot to teach indigenous organisations about how to encourage really lively activity and participation.

Other day centres and clubs
The Jewish community, with its very long-established tradition of care for its older members, provides an example of the wide range of specialist services which can be developed, given the influence and encouragement of national or local voluntary organisations such as the various Jewish Welfare Boards, the League of Jewish Women and the Jewish Blind Society. These initiatives range in scale from small 'friendship clubs' meeting on only one afternoon a week, usually in premises attached to a synagogue and providing light refreshments, but not a cooked meal (no 31) to local day centres providing meals and activities (no 33), up to really large-scale projects such as Michael Sobell House (no 34) which offers an immense range of activity and caters for nearly 250 people a day. Also described in Appendix 1 is the flourishing Cypriot Elderly and Handicapped Group in Haringey (no 30) and, as was noted above, plans are being made to develop centres for Poles (see p. 37) Chinese (see p. 40) and Irish (see p. 23) people. The fact that such disparate groups are developing centres which operate in a basically similar way is some indication that, however it is best met, this is a need which is strongly felt and will continue for many years.

Staffing
Staffing levels
The sense of being understaffed to meet demand was expressed at almost every centre where paid staff were employed. The pressures and responsibilities of running a voluntary day care project are very heavy. They include those related to running the centre, such as worrying about the clients, arranging activities, managing staff and volunteers, mobilising equipment and resources, operating a counselling and advice service, and developing outreach into people's own homes. But they also include duties involved in running the organisation, such as relating to the management committee, applying for funding, liaising with other organisations and conforming to council requirements in administrative, financial, personnel, planning and other terms. One worker said that 'it felt like being cut with knives' when he was unable to give time to individual requests for help and attention because of the demands of running the organisation. The activities described above cannot be effectively provided with less than three people employed at professional level, plus cooking, caretaking, secretarial and transport back-up, but very few of the organisations visited had core funding for staffing of this kind. Once a service is started, the pressure to expand it seems to be inexorable: more and more time needs to be given to information and counselling; to lengthy battles with officialdom on behalf of clients; to providing care services for temporarily ill or housebound people; and to building bridges with statutory services of all kinds.

Staff pay and conditions
Pay and conditions of service do not reflect these responsibilities. A report by the Department of the Environment on voluntary projects funded by Urban Aid in Birmingham and the London Borough of Fulham & Hammersmith[1] found that pay levels were often low in relation both to hours worked and to salary scales applying to colleagues in statutory services. Additional benefits such as superannuation arrangements were rarely found outside larger organisations that had developed specific conditions of service. Staffing levels made no allowance for sickness or prolonged absence, and no facility existed for the rapid authorisation of funding for temporary staff or, in appropriate cases, for making local authority staff available on loan. A report, *Inner cities policy and ethnic minorities*, by the School of Advanced Urban Studies[2] at Bristol points out that 'at the initial stage of a project, the determination of salary grades will not be able to take account of project development and the potential increased responsibilities for workers as projects grow and diversify. There are therefore often

problems in the second and subsequent years of work, not only over the award of increments, but also over the re-negotiation of salary levels and conditions of service'. If the role of the voluntary sector is to be taken seriously, it is important that staff employed in it are not treated as second-rate professionals who are fit subjects for exploitation. People cannot be expected to give of their best if they are suffering from a chronic sense of injustice, and experienced and qualified workers will choose to go elsewhere.

Staff support and training
Very few of the organisers in clubs and day centres visited had had any professional training for the role. In the Asian schemes they were typically middle-aged professional men whose backgrounds included teaching, accountancy, constructional engineering and commerce. In the Afro-Caribbean centres, the organisers tended to be middle-aged women who were leaders within their own community, but who also seldom had formal training in any aspects of this complex field. This lack of preparatory training is not usually compensated for by in-service opportunities for self-assessment and development. The DoE study quoted found that:

'Opportunities for the worker to discuss the efficiency and effectiveness of his work with someone not directly involved on a day-to-day basis—but who was nevertheless knowledgeable in the appropriate field—were limited. We found instances where the project worker would have positively welcomed some form of objective assessment of his or her activities, not to mention the encouragement or re-direction that might have resulted. The effects of sometimes infrequent contact with management committees or colleagues, combined with the comparative isolation of many projects, should not be underestimated.

We encountered surprisingly few instances where individuals had been able to attend development courses or meetings relevant to their work, sometimes due to a lack of awareness of their existence, sometimes to pressure of work—whichever is the case, it is not an auspicious sign for the promotion of good standards in the future.

We would like to see greater use of some form of job description against which an objective assessment could take place and by which the workers could be quite clear about their terms of reference. The possibility of having a suitably qualified individual with whom a project worker could discuss his or her work, and the provision of organised opportunities for debate with peers, are two issues that we feel warrant further consideration by the CVSs and the local authorities. The growth and development of projects cannot take place without the commensurate development of those responsible for running them. To this end we consider that current information on availability of both technical and non-technical training is an area of which all projects should be aware.'[3]

There is a lot of scope for local authorities to offer basic induction training about the nature and range of their services to new employees in day centres, as Nottingham Social Services Department has recently arranged to do for the two MSC staff joining the Indian Community Day Centre (no 11). Established voluntary organisations such as Age Concern and the Citizens Advice Bureaux could also share their training facilities. In places where there are a large number of initiatives within a relatively small area organisations could perhaps run training days on various aspects of day centre management, as London's Standing Conference of Ethnic Minority Senior Citizens plans to do.[4] However, voluntary organisations which have fought to achieve an independent existence often fear that support services offered by a local authority or 'umbrella' organisation will threaten their autonomy. Immense care needs to be taken to ensure that any offer of training or support is consistent, trustworthy and, if possible, not too closely associated with the funding body.

Management styles
The clubs and day centres visited represented as wide a range of management methods and styles as would be found in indigenous voluntary organisations. Some have a managing committee which is not elected by the user members, though there may be members' committees to fund-raise or arrange events and members may be represented on the main committee. Some have a committee directly responsible to the membership; some are offshoots of a community centre, religious body or other organisation and have no independent management, and so on. The variations do not seem to make a great deal of difference in practice, and the personalities of those mainly involved with running the centre or club appear to be of much more importance than the constitutional arrangements. However, when, as often is the case, a service owes its existence primarily to one person's vision, determination and hard work, there is a potential tension between the exercise of such leadership and the development of democratic decision-making and shared responsibility. The most successful initiatives seem to be those in

which leadership skills are deliberately exercised to encourage self-determination and self-help.

Provision of facilities for both sexes
The Jewish and Afro-Caribbean centres seem to be used by many more women than men. One reason for this may be that they have initially been set up and run by women and it might help to bring in more men at management and volunteer level to encourage others to come in as users. Other reasons must, of course, be the greater longevity of women and the fact that there is less need for companionship at a day centre when both partners in a marriage are alive. Certainly there are many lonely, bored and isolated men in both communities and a determined effort is needed to provide occupations and facilities which would help to attract them. This implies the need for increased space and storage facilities, and funds for providing tools and raw materials, though the Senior Citizens Friendly Association in Birmingham (no 26) shows what can be done even with very limited facilities.

Conversely, women are very badly catered for in most of the Asian Centres visited, and nowhere except Scope Southall (no 1) has there been any serious attempt to provide separate but equal facilities. Some of those consulted in the course of preparing this report remain convinced that older Asian women are, in general, too unaccustomed to going out to make use of any facility which might be provided and that their social needs are adequately met in the home. Others are equally convinced that if the facilities are acceptable, transport is available and time and trouble are taken to get to know such women in their own homes, they could be persuaded to make the attempt and that this would help to meet a really desperate need for relief from loneliness, boredom and depression. Certainly, the odd examples of successful provision for women (see nos 1, 4, 8, 10, 11) support this view, though the particular needs of each Asian group would, of course, have to be identified and recognised. At present, the numerical preponderance of men over women in the older Asian age groups has served to limit demand, but the generation now becoming old will have a much higher proportion of women and it is essential that their needs be catered for.

It is very noticeable, though scarcely surprising, what a difference having a female member of staff makes in encouraging women to use the facilities, and a number of centres which do not already have a woman staff member are planning to appoint one as part of their expansion.

Age-range
Many of the centres visited set 50 as the age of eligibility for admission. Others had no fixed rule and relied on self-selection. Only Milap Southall (no 2) had a rigorous policy of excluding people under 60 unless they were also physically disabled, in which case they were accepted at 55. This flexibility about age of admission illustrates the importance of not forcing services for older members of ethnic minorities into a mould which imitates established practice, regardless of its appropriateness to the community concerned—or indeed its appropriateness in general. The lower age limit which operates in traditional clubs and day centres is usually the 60/65 pensionable age, but this is making less and less sense in view of the increasing numbers of unemployed middle-aged people. Because of their low income and lack of daytime occupation, these people are just as much in need of clubs and day centres as pensioners are, and perhaps *all* service providers should consider following the lead of the ethnic minority voluntary organisations and accept people from 50. On the other hand, it should be noted that some local authority informants said that they would find it difficult to justify contributing funds to provide services for relatively young people when they were not able adequately to meet the needs of people in extreme old age. It may also be that as some members of the immigrant generation become very frail and require a very supportive environment, the ethnic minority service providers will find that they cannot look after them properly while also catering for younger and more active people, and that these would be better catered for separately. It will be of interest to see how policy develops in this regard.

Transport
Inevitably, lack of suitable transport was a major complaint in many of the centres visited, and it was clear that when adequate facilities were available they made a great deal of difference, enabling disabled people and people living at a distance to be brought in, and meals to be taken to housebound people and outings to be arranged. In some cases, vehicles were successfully shared with a youth group (no 17), or with a Community Transport operation (no 5). In Lambeth, a Dial-a-Ride service can provide transport, but this can only be used by people who have a telephone. Help with transport is one area in which assistance from established voluntary organisations is valued. Brent Age Concern, for example, has helped local organisations to obtain their own vehicles through Opportunities for Volunteering or Help the Aged; Hackney Pensioners' Link provides transport once a month to

bring disabled people to the HEADS club (no 25), and Tottenham Old Peoples' Welfare provides transport for a disabled West Indian Club. Nottinghamshire Social Services was the only local authority which used its own vehicles to take people to specialist lunch clubs and to the day centre run by the Indian Community Association (no 11). This was much appreciated, but the centre's catchment area covers the whole city and another vehicle was very badly needed to bring the service to an adequate standard.

Transport issues are, of course, closely tied up with the size of the undertaking and its catchment area. Some informants felt strongly that small local centres cannot provide the necessary range of facilities and that what are required are large purpose-built centres employing professional health and welfare staff and serving a wide catchment area. Advocates of small-scale provision argue that many people are prepared to use a small, local, friendly centre when they would not be prepared to travel a considerable distance to a large and more impersonal facility.

In either case, the transport required is a fundamental consideration when an appropriate catchment area is being worked out and it needs to be tackled from the start when service provision is being planned. This is especially important when a centre is seeking to cater for those Asian women who are unable to leave their homes to attend a centre unless transport can be provided.

Revenue funding
Reference has already been made to the inadequate staffing levels resulting from insufficient core funding which were characteristic of most of the projects visited. In some cases, efforts are made to increase the staff provided by an urban aid grant by the use of workers paid by the Manpower Services Commission (MSC). This is an inherently unsatisfactory practice because MSC employees are normally only allowed to stay for a year, so they leave almost as soon as they are able to take real responsibility. Also constant staff turnover is distressing to elderly people. Other drawbacks are that funding can be withdrawn at a week's notice if the MSC become dissatisfied for any reason, as happened with Scope Southall (no 1). Also, continued funding is never guaranteed because government policy in relation to MSC activity changes frequently and has now become unfavourable towards using MSC employees in the voluntary services. In spite of these drawbacks, however, some organisations such as the West Indian Women's Association in Brent (no 17). the United Caribbean Association in Leeds (no 29) and the

Wesleyan Holiness Church in Birmingham (no 27) are making successful use of considerable numbers of MSC staff.

Another potential solution to meeting staff costs is for the local authority to become the employer and apply to the Home Office for 75 per cent of the employee's salary under Section 11 of the Local Government Act 1966. (See p 140 for further details). This ploy had only been used in one of the centres visited—the Asian Day Centre in Leeds (no 12)—and it was adopted when funding from the Commission for Racial Equality (CRE) ran out. The circumstances were rather exceptional in this case, in that the centre meets on council premises and was set up in close association with staff of the social services department. The Community Relations Council was responsible for the original appointment, but there was no local management committee and no-one seemed to feel threatened by the new arrangement. In situations where the present employer is a strongly independent voluntary organisation, it seems likely that both the Home Office and the organisation concerned might be reluctant to consider this solution. It is, however, worth bearing in mind as a possibility.

In the London area, many organisations have turned to the Greater London Council (GLC) for help, and the abolition of the GLC and the metropolitan counties will be a serious blow to them. Organisations also turn to sources such as Opportunities for Volunteering and other specialist funds, but this may result in 'skewing' their activities to meet the criteria of the fund concerned.

For most of the organisations visited, the prime source of revenue funding was some form of urban aid, and as chapter 10 spells out in detail, this is only provided for a limited period and is by no means certain of renewal. The original intention behind the urban aid concept was that local authorities should take projects which had proved their value into mainstream funding, but in a time of rate-capping and retrenchment, this too cannot be guaranteed and there is a very real danger of initiatives losing their funding altogether. At best, staff are having to spend far too much time and energy pursuing grant applications when they are needed to run the service concerned. In CPA's view, local authorities should consider whether any specialist service at risk is in fact the equivalent of the council service available to indigenous elderly people. If so, the authority concerned would, CPA believes, have a moral duty to guarantee continued funding. It might attempt to secure this through backing a further urban aid application, or by applying for

Section 11 money, but if such sources should fail there would be no equitable alternative to taking the project into mainstream funding. If, because of the recession and government pressure to keep spending down, mainstream resources were insufficient, it would be essential to make sure that the facilities provided for ethnic groups did not suffer more than those available to the indigenous community.

Selection of projects for funding

The author of this report received much critical comment from both local authority staff and voluntary organisations on the process of obtaining grant aid from the Urban Programme. Organisers of projects complained that it was those who were most articulate or who had personal contact with councillors who got all the money, and that communities who needed most help might in fact get least. There was a frequent plea for more open and better consultative processes which gave an opportunity for members of the minority communities to speak for themselves about their needs rather than relying on self-styled 'community leaders' whose views might be ill-informed, self-serving or biased. On the local government side, officers often felt that they themselves were not adequately consulted during the decision-making process and that the time schedule made it impossible for them to consult with the communities as much as they would like to. Particular difficulties can arise when the programme authority is the district council responsible for an inner city area, but the project concerned primarily relates to social services managed by a county council. There are also problems when the voluntary organisation concerned straddles various activities and therefore a number of committees and even more than one authority. See, for example, the difficulty which the All Moslem Women and Children Association in Brent (no 8) has had in obtaining funding for its work.

These are not new problems. The authors of *The politics of positive discrimination*[5] found, in their review of the first ten years of the Urban Programme, that voluntary agencies felt there was inadequate machinery for involving them in the grant-making process; that agencies 'in the know' were favoured; that there was not enough time for consultation; and that the statutory authorities distrusted them. The means of distributing central government circulars setting out current rules and priorities for making an application came in for particular criticism. Many agencies either received the circular too late to take effective action before the deadline, did not receive it at all, or heard about it only on the grapevine. It was suggested that in some cases this amounted to 'a rationing of funds by ignorance'—a form of discrimination to which the ethnic minority voluntary agencies are particularly vulnerable because of their isolation from the mainstream.

It is one thing to advocate proper consultation and clear and open decision-making and quite another to achieve it. A recent study[6] of attempts in Manchester to put into practice the ideal of partnership with local people as 'a necessary means to the regeneration of the inner areas and an end in its own right' found what one reviewer summed up as 'a sorry tale of mismatch of perceptions, mistrust between the two sectors and a build-up of tensions which do not seem to have found a productive release and this in spite of, or perhaps because of, a particularly ambitious attempt to provide consultative mechanisms'. Some progress is being made, as the School of Advanced Urban Studies (SAUS) report points out, but much more needs to be done both in setting up mechanisms for communicating with the minority communities at grass roots level rather than through CRCs and CVSs, and in simplifying and de-mystifying the grant application process. The SAUS report recommends a simplified application procedure, possibly using a model form developed by the NCVO and local authority associations; widespread publicity about the programme; information about sources of help in drawing up an application; careful provision of information to applicants about the process and rationale of the decision-making procedure; and the appointment of Project Development Officers paid by Section 11 funding to help the ethnic minorities to use the programme. These procedures, it says, should be accompanied by continuing analysis of 'the proportion of funds allocated to black projects, the type of black projects funded and not funded; the status of black groups receiving funds (established versus new); the effect on groups of getting a grant; the impact of DoE guidance on potential for funding black groups; the impact of time expiry pressures on funding; the conflicts within communities arising from some groups getting money and others not; and the implementation of black projects'.[7]

Premises
As has already been noted, clubs and day centres for older members of ethnic minorities are often established in run-down, second- or third-rate premises which are not suitable for severely disabled people and are often lacking in room for storage and space for constructive activities. Many informants expressed bitterness at what they felt to be lack of equal treatment compared with the facilities made available to white clubs, and there were also reports of racial

discrimination against groups trying to obtain shared use of a community centre. For example, Pensioners Link in Haringey said that they had helped a West Indian weekly club to gain entry to a local community centre, but its members were experiencing hostility from the caretaker and from members of a club which met in the afternoon of the same day. When capital is made available through urban aid to provide premises, the amount is often quite inadequate for the purpose so that either an unsuitable building has to be accepted or no progress can be made with the project.

Some very large sums are sometimes provided to build or adapt a community centre for a particular ethnic group, but all too often not enough trouble is taken to ensure that the design of the building is suitable to meet a range of needs which includes those of elderly people. Various informants expressed disquiet because they believed that religious organisations had been given grants to build or adapt community centres which were then primarily used for religious purposes. There is also a danger of such centres being taken over by a clique which is not representative of all the sectors of the community concerned. Another problem with capital grant-giving for ethnic minority community centres is that there is often insufficient associated revenue funding. The assumption is that running costs can be met from lettings, but without proper core staffing for administration and management this is not possible.

Local authorities which try to meet their obligations by providing decent premises from mainstream funding may run into political opposition. For example, in Lewisham plans for the Calabash Centre (no 14) were opposed by a petition from residents in the street concerned, who claimed that it would reduce the value of their property, was 'blatant discrimination against whites', would cause an increase in vehicle traffic and would duplicate facilities provided elsewhere.

The whole process of acquiring premises is one of great complexity as the SAUS report quoted above explains:

'The most consistent problems of implementation arise in relation to the acquisition, renovation and occupancy of premises. Most authorities, firstly, experience a dearth of suitable premises for community groups. Older industrial premises and redundant churches and schools offer major opportunities for conversion, but renovation costs are normally high and legal negotiations complex. Secondly, there are a number of examples of slow bureaucratic practice in local authority departments, notably associated with planning, development control and building regulations, which hinder further the timely supply of premises for community activities. Much of this delay arises from the traditional values of some local government departments—estates and planning are commonly cast as villains—which are simply not flexible enough to respond to the demands of community groups. The latter reflect a profoundly different cultural style of operation and approach compared to that of most local authorities. For example, development control processes rely heavily on the norms of 'conforming' uses and there are numerous instances where community centres, religious activities, workshop initiatives and so on are inhibited by planning considerations. In dealing with building professionals, ie surveyors, architects, valuers, etc., inexperienced community groups are often ill-equipped to contradict professional views on leasing arrangements, improvements, maintenance and management. Some authorities (eg Brent and Hackney) have reviewed their policy towards buildings for community groups and we recommend that all local authorities should carry out a review of policies towards premises with the concerns of ethnic minorities in mind.

Black groups, particularly West Indian groups, are keen to preserve their right to self-determination and self-help. Ownership or 'perceived ownership' of premises or of a minimum space in a building is therefore vital to such groups. It is sometimes not sufficient simply to provide leased premises and hand over the keys to a group who desire to operate independently from the bureaucracy and who are sensitive to the threat of continuing local authority intervention and control. Some local authorities are reluctant for technical/legal/accountability considerations to sell premises freehold. Black groups in particular may be perceived as a high risk investment, the ultimate risk being that the group will fold up, cease to operate and make a profit from the sale of the premises. This risk can, of course, easily be overcome by the insertion of covenants or placing a charge which restricts the sale of the building. There is a further problem surrounding the use of multi-occupied premises and the availability of secure rooms or cupboard space for group equipment. Not merely because equipment may represent a group's main asset, but also because secure, independent space is, as argued above, a prerequisite for group development, many groups are unwilling to share premises. The fear of incompatibility between occupants thus reinforces the need for, and tendency towards, the provision of separate premises for individual black groups rather than multi-occupied (and possibly multi-cultural) premises.'[8]

Clearly, much more careful consideration needs to be given to this area than it has received and the provision of premises needs thought early in the planning stage of any project.

Continuing support and evaluation
The local authority officers and the published reports consulted in the course of this study agree that there is not nearly enough systematic evaluation of ethnic minority projects. However, as several people pointed out, this is also true of both local authority provision and established voluntary services, and there is a very real danger of stricter standards being enforced for new ethnic initiatives than for indigenous and well-established services. *All* developments need monitoring to ascertain what service they are providing and to whom, what the customer thinks of it, and how far it has been successful in encouraging local involvement and tapping hidden resources. One difficulty is that grants seldom allow staff time for such evaluation. Another problem is that assessment inevitably becomes confused with the justification of continued financial support, and the organisation concerned is therefore in a defensive position in which it has to paint as bright a picture as possible rather than look honestly at what is happening and what can be learned from it. It would be helpful if each local authority attached to its notification of grant approval a letter stating clearly why the project had been approved and what the money was being provided for— for example, is it to tackle a particular area of concern or gap in provision; to meet the need of some particular ethnic minority group, or to experiment with an innovative way of providing a service? If the objective was clearly laid down, evaluation could focus on how far the project was succeeding in meeting its stated purpose and, if it was moving away from it, how and why this was happening. Perhaps, the holding of 'review days' could be built into the grant approval, and these could be attended by the service providers, the service users, the local authority funders and interested local groups. Such evaluations should be seen as serving a much more creative purpose than a 'school report' type of assessment and, as was noted above, be a condition of *all* grants.

It is particularly important than an agreed review is carried out at the beginning of the year in which the grant runs out, so that careful unhurried consideration can be given to the project's future and any recommendation for mainstream funding or further urban programme support be made. All this does, of course, take time and energy, and one local authority officer suggested that it is unlikely to happen because it is uncomfortable to know too clearly how successful or unsuccessful projects have been. He also suggested that 'local authorities don't mind too much anyway, because it is only 25 per cent of their money'. But in a situation where every penny matters, it is clearly vital that we know what is being funded, why it is being funded and with what success.

Most authorities at present rely for their continuing contact with projects on a liaison officer—usually a local authority employee whose ordinary work relates to the purpose of the voluntary organisation in some way. However, as one report demonstrates in detail,[9] there is a good deal of confusion about the proper role of liaison officers and the separate administrative, professional, managerial and support functions which they are often expected to perform. If, as usually happens, they sit on the management committee, they may be uncertain whether they are there to serve the organisation or the council, and their presence may be seen as an attack on the organisation's autonomy and independence rather than as a means of tapping council expertise and resources. There is certainly a need for clear thinking about their role, and for them to have senior colleagues with whom they can consult and who can take over any trouble-shooting that might be necessary.

Conclusion
This chapter has concentrated on the problems and limitations of voluntary clubs and day centres as they operate at present, and their difficulties in terms of funding, staffing, transport and premises, because these are matters which local authorities, 'umbrella' voluntary organisations and the central government funding authorities could and should be doing something about. It would, however, be misleading to leave the subject without again emphasising not only their immense potential but their achievement in providing for elderly members of ethnic minority groups. The service which they provide is valuable in terms of offering a place in which to relax, enjoy oneself, feel at home, make friends and forget one's troubles. But it is also extremely important as a base for many other kinds of activity—for learning languages and new skills, getting trustworthy information and advice, eating palatable and nourishing food, going on trips and outings, and making contact with supporters who can be trusted also to give help in the home.

The next chapter in this report spells out in more detail how these activities interact with local authority mainstream services and how these services can be developed so that they can be offered in genuine co-operation with the ethnic minority groups. Such co-operation demands an articulation of the needs of elderly people in particular communities, so that the authority concerned can be made more aware and more responsive. It is in the clubs and day centres that elderly people have a chance to state their needs and find a platform from which they can express them clearly. If consultation in service development is to mean anything, there is a duty on the management, staff and members of clubs and day centres to use them for this purpose, and a duty on the local authority concerned to ensure that what is said is seriously considered and taken into account in policy development.

SUMMARY OF ACTION REQUIRED

Action by ethnic minority groups
1. Campaign for equitable funding of specialist services which provide an appropriate equivalent to services available to indigenous elderly people.
2. Set up appropriate services where they do not exist at present.
3. Use clubs and day centres as a means of articulating the needs of their members in relation to mainstream services.
4. Give careful thought at the planning stage to:
    staff roles, management, support and training
    involvement of members in decision making
    catchment area and transport provision
    means of providing an equal service to both sexes
    age limits
    forward thinking in relation to future funding
    monitoring and evaluation.

Action by local authorities
1. Accept responsibility for funding and supporting initiatives which provide a service equivalent to that used by the indigenous population.
2. Make premises and facilities used by the indigenous population as accessible as possible to ethnic minority groups.
3. Look at facilities offered to the indigenous population afresh in the light of ethnic minority initiatives, with particular reference to age limits, activities and management styles.
4. Think through and state policy in relation to:
    consultation with club members, staff and management

groups about policies and priorities relating to elderly members of the community concerned

realistic staff levels, staff pay and training facilities in clubs and centres

appropriate management structures

equitable use of club and centre facilities in relation to sex, age and religion

equitable use of local authority transport facilities

use of Section 11 funding to supplement staff levels or provide ancillary support and liaison

means of informing ethnic minority organisations about the process of applying for urban aid

means of assisting organisations to obtain suitable premises

means of ensuring continuing support and evaluation.

Action by central government

1. Be consistent in encouraging ethnic minority voluntary initiatives in this field through urban aid grants.
2. Accept that revenue funding will need to increase as new initiatives are set up and established ones expand.
3. Accept the use of Section 11 funding to encourage development of specialist centres and clubs.
4. Improve procedures in the urban aid process.

REFERENCES

1. Stuart Elliott, Graham Lomas, Alan Riddell, *Community projects review: a review of voluntary projects receiving Urban Programme funding,* Department of the Environment, London, 1984.
2. Murray Stewart and Gill Whitting, *Ethnic minorities and the Urban Programme.* Occasional Paper No. 9, School of Advanced Urban Studies, University of Bristol, 1983.
3. See ref. 1.
4. The Standing Conference of Ethnic Minority Senior Citizens, *Ethnic minority senior citizens: a first report,* London, 1984
5. John Edwards and Richard Batley, *The politics of positive discrimination: an evaluation of the Urban Programme 1967–77,* Tavistock Publications. London, 1978.
6. Gwyndaf Williams, *Inner city policy: a partnership with the voluntary sector,* Bedford Square Press, London 1983.
7. See ref. 2.
8. Ibid.
9. *Working together: partnerships in local social service;* compiled by a working party convened by the Association of Metropolitan Authorities, the National Council for Voluntary Organisations, and the Association of County Councils, London, Bedford Square Press/NCVO, 1981.

6 Provision of other services

Introduction

The previous chapter sketched the progress made by various ethnic minority groups in setting up day centres and clubs to meet the particular needs of various groups of older people for social contact and support. Ethnic minority initiatives are, however, by no means confined to simple provision of day centres and clubs. Members of the various communities are becoming increasingly concerned about the needs of elderly people for domiciliary support, meals-on-wheels, and reliable information and advice, and as we have seen, clubs and day centres are being used as springboards for the development of these kinds of services. There is tremendous scope for the ethnic minority communities to work closely with local authorities to make use of mainstream facilities and resources and to press for their development to meet particular needs. This chapter looks at voluntary initiatives which are already off the ground and their relationship with local authority services.

Domiciliary support and care

Home help is one of the main pillars of support for elderly people in our society, but is extremely difficult to provide in an acceptable way for people of other languages, creeds and customs. The AFFOR study in Birmingham[1] found that, while 19 per cent of their European sample received home help, only nine per cent of the Afro-Caribbeans and no Asians did so. Ninety-four per cent of the Europeans knew of the service, as did 83 per cent of Afro-Caribbeans, but only 19 per cent of the Asians. No data are available for other ethnic minority groups: the impression obtained from service providers is that Jewish and Irish elderly people make normal use of the service (except for the Hasidic Jewish sects), but that there is a continuous struggle to cross the language barriers in providing services for European and Cypriot immigrants.

Poor take-up is also due to other factors. The AFFOR study found that 34 per cent of the Asian sample said they would not use the home help service if they needed help because their families would care for them, and in some areas at least the ethnic minority population has not aged sufficiently to make an extensive demand on the service. Thus, 87 per cent of the Afro-Caribbeans in the AFFOR study said that they would use the service if they needed it and similar willingness was expressed in the Nottinghamshire survey.[2] This may mean overcoming considerable personal reluctance, however. Cooper's detailed study of Afro-Caribbean elders found 'There seemed to be a general feeling amongst the respondents that the English do not share their standards of hygiene. In several cases, women who had witnessed the preparation of food at their places of work were horrified, for example, that meat might be cooked without having been washed. Although they did not say very much on the subject, I suspect to spare my feelings, I felt that it was of considerable significance to them.'[3] Similarly, members of the West Indian Senior Citizens Club in Haringey (no 23 in Appendix 1) expressed disgust to the author of this report that television advertisements for washing-up liquid showed crockery being dried without being rinsed in clear water. Where the helper is of exactly the same ethnic background as the client, this particular problem is less likely to arise, but different standards and customs arising from the generation gap can still create problems.

Reluctance to accept some help from an outsider may also arise from suspicion, fear and shame, and this is worrying because the people who need the service most may be excluding themselves from it. This view is put forward with great conviction by Lynn Grant, the Afro-Caribbean chairwoman and founder of the Harlesden Community Care project in Brent. She says that there are many elderly Afro-Caribbeans in the area who receive no support from their families and who are terrified of bringing their plight to official notice because they fear being put into residential care, which they equate with a West Indian 'poorhouse' and consider a social disgrace. They are also ashamed to let outsiders see their low standard of living and also believe (with justification) that asking for help will mean enquiries about their income—'they will only want to know how much I have saved'. These people, Lynn Grant says, have virtually given up. They have a sense of failure and uselessness which compounds their physical disabilities and generates a social isolation which they no longer try to overcome. Persuading them to accept help, even from a member of their own community, takes much patience and tact. The project has identified forty such people in the Harlesden area, mainly through the churches, knocking on doors and asking around, and ten volunteers have been recruited who provide domestic help and personal care. Having proved the need, the project is now seeking funding to pay one full-time organiser and two part-time workers to provide a stable backbone for the service, but will continue to use volunteers as well, particularly at evenings and weekends.

The Harlesden Community Care project is unique, but other organisations are using clubs and day centres as a base from which they can extend their work into people's own homes. The United Caribbean Association in Birmingham (no 29) puts much emphasis on giving domiciliary care when needed as well as on providing a bridge between the client and statutory services. Similarly, the organiser of the Cottage of Content Day Care Centre, also in Birmingham (no 28) sees domiciliary support as an important part of her role. She supplements, but does not supplant, the statutory home help service, and tries to provide companionship as well as practical help. Rather different in character is a voluntary visiting service being developed in association with the Pepper Pot Club in North Kensington (no 24). This uses funds from the Opportunities for Volunteering scheme to take on six unemployed people to develop neighbourhood work, including minor decorating, looking after window-boxes, reading aloud and talking. These volunteers do not, however, provide personal care and they report the need for such help rather than trying to meet it. The club's organiser, Pansy Jeffrey, emphasises the importance of not using volunteers in a way which crosses professional boundaries and of being tactful in bringing need to official notice without appearing to be too critical. Many other clubs and centres in all the ethnic groups under review are beginning to extend similar support to housebound or temporarily-ill members, or express the wish to do so, but are frustrated by lack of funds and demands on the time of the organiser. It is clear that there is an immense amount of scope for development both in providing services within the communities and in bridge-building between potential clients and the statutory services.

The statutory authorities can help the process by making a particular effort to employ home helps and home help organisers from the appropriate ethnic groups. There are various ways in which this can be done. One possibility is to delegate the responsibility for recruiting and deploying home helps for a particular community to some organisation within that community. This gets over the considerable difficulty which local authorities have in encouraging recruits with the right qualifications to come forward, and in matching them appropriately with clients—particularly amongst Asians. Anil Bhalla in Birmingham, for example, (see p. 47) would like to see the advisory committee with which he works develop into an Asian Elders Management Committee with responsibility for providing specialist services, including home help, on behalf of the statutory authority. It appears that the Jewish Welfare Board has been used successfully in this way to provide Jewish home helps in some London boroughs, and a similar arrangement has also been established by the London Borough of Hackney and the Hasidic sects. The problem with this solution is that it presupposes the existence of an organisation with the necessary management skills and community contacts to operate such a service to the standard required, and it cuts off the specialist home helps from the relationship with the other domiciliary services and the rest of the social services department which they ought to enjoy. There may also be problems over travelling time and costs to meet the needs of a relatively small number of people in a large city.

Another approach is to make a really serious effort to recruit home helps from the appropriate communities into the statutory service. This would not only create a pool of workers who have the requisite social and language skills, but also provide equal opportunity of employment to members of the ethnic communities. This approach has been followed with success in the Foleshill area of Coventry. Here the social services team leader (who is himself Asian) spread news of a recruitment drive through cleaners at the Family Centre (the area office), local community groups and other word-of-mouth information channels. He would also have used shop-window advertising if this had proved necessary. All those who showed interest were invited to a group information-giving session at which the nature of the job was explained and those who were evidently unsuitable were weeded out. An unusually large shortlist was left, however, and these were carefully interviewed and asked about attitudes to racial differences, undertaking menial tasks, working for members of other castes and ethnic groups, and working for members of the opposite sex. Such unusually careful interviewing is seen as essential in recruiting people to work in an ethnically mixed community, as it is impossible to judge suitability on the basis of the very inadequate information provided in the application forms. This approach has proved to be very successful in enabling balanced and suitable recruitment, but it is expensive in terms of time and has required considerable bending of the rules of employment procedures. It also implies the availability of senior staff who know what they are doing and can communicate with applicants in a sensitive way. No other authorities are known to have taken this amount of trouble, but many have given up relying on word-of-mouth publicity which tended to bring in friends of existing staff and are advertising vacancies in the ethnic press as well as the local English language newspapers. This approach does not seem to have been very successful, however, and much more use could be made of the existing community organisations and leaders to encourage suitable applicants to come forward.

Having recruited home helps from various ethnic backgrounds, how do you deploy them within a generalist service? This is by no means a simple issue. As was noted above, clients from a particular group may be too scattered to make it economic to allow a home help to work only with clients of her own ethnic background and, in any case, the complexity of the immigrant population makes it difficult to achieve exact matching. West Indian immigrants from different islands—perhaps 1,000 miles apart—may have very different customs and speak different versions of English, for example, or an Asian with the right language skills might be of a different faith or caste from a potential client; and a Polish home help might be no better at communicating with a Hungarian client than a member of the indigenous population. In some situations, indeed, a white English worker might be more acceptable to the client, in spite of language and cultural differences, than someone who was near, but not near enough, to the client's own background. Also any attempt at ethnic matching brings with it the danger of implying that ethnic minority clients are not good enough for indigenous home helps, and ethnic minority home helps are not good enough for indigenous clients. There is also the fact that many elderly Anglo-Saxons may prefer to have a home help of their own culture. If the local authority is doing its utmost to provide acceptable services to the minority groups, has it any right to deny such a right to the indigenous population? On the other hand, does the authority have the right to permit clients to insist on a service which will result in racially discriminatory employment practices? Any rule-of-thumb solution is bound to be unjust and unsatisfactory, and the essential starting point is to have a pool of employees who are sufficiently varied in ethnic background to make it possible to match client to helper in a way which takes account of particular needs and abilities in each case. Further, it is important that methods of recruitment and deployment should be thought through with representative groups in the communities concerned, so that conflicting principles can be spelled out and compromises openly agreed. The local authority can then link up with initiatives arising from the communities both to provide ancillary domiciliary services and to encourage full and proper use of the statutory service.

Specialist meals services
Provision of acceptable and nutritious food has been an underlying theme throughout this report. A good lunch is basic to any provision of full day-centre facilities. Nutrition is a key aspect of maintaining good health; the provision of acceptable food is an important aspect of hospital treatment; day-time homelessness and lack of adequate cooking facilities are aspects of housing need which encourage malnutrition; and the provision of meals is a basic

part of domiciliary care. In spite of its importance, however, few authorities have given really serious attention to providing acceptable meals for elderly members of the main ethnic minority communities and at the time of writing only Brent has attempted to give equal weight to the needs of the Jewish, Asian and Afro-Caribbean populations.

It is admittedly not easy to provide such a service and requires close and continuing consultation with members of the communities concerned, as well as great care to ensure that the right diet is matched to the right religious group. Some of the complexities of the Asian diet are outlined in one of a series of articles on Asians in hospital published by the *Health and Social Service Journal.* The authors explain that:

'Hindu attitudes to food are based on respect for all forms of life and the belief that man does not have the right to take other lives to sustain his own. Most Hindus follow a vegetarian diet and do not eat meat, fish, eggs or any of their products. They rely mainly on combinations of vegetable protein, such as chapattis, or rice and pulses, and on dairy products. They do not generally drink alcohol. Even those Hindus who eat meat do not generally eat beef, since the cow is venerated as a sacred symbol of gentleness and loving motherhood.

Many Sikhs, particularly women, eat a vegetarian diet based on Hindu restrictions. Even Sikhs who eat meat will not generally eat beef. Devout Sikhs regard alcohol as a harmful stimulant.

Muslim dietary restrictions are clearly specified in the Quran. Muslims may not eat pork or pork products such as lard, bacon or sausages. They may only eat halal (permitted) meat that has been specially killed and blessed. Any meat products must also be halal. This includes meat-based stocks, meat extracts, margarines, and so on. Kosher meat is acceptable to Muslims. Alcohol is strictly forbidden.'[4]

According to this article further information is available in a handbook published by the DHSS Catering and Dietetic Branch, entitled *Catering for minority groups,* and a training kit on Asian foods and diets is now available from the National Extension College.

Catering adequately for the various Asian groups may be the most complex challenge, but the special needs of the other communities are of equal importance. We have seen, for example, how strongly elderly Afro-Caribbeans may feel about hygiene in food preparation. Middle-aged and younger Afro-Caribbeans may now have become accustomed to English food and find West Indian food too expensive and too time-consuming to prepare except on special occasions, but most older people still have a very strong preference for traditional dishes and the same is true for the Cypriot community. Orthodox Jewish people conform to strict regulations which govern not only how meat is killed but ingredients, methods of preparation and what foods may or may not be eaten together. All communities have particular festivals and fasts and traditional foods associated with them.

There are a number of ways of meeting these diverse needs and it seems likely that different ones should be employed in different situations. Where there is an established day centre with good cooking facilities, it may be most acceptable and cost-effective to pay for a cook to prepare food on the premises and take extra meals to housebound clients in the neighbourhood. The Afro-Caribbean clubs and centres normally prepare food on the premises. This may be because they have women members, organisers and volunteers who can share in the work and also because there is not likely to be an alternative (Afro-Caribbean restaurants from which food could be bought in are few and far between, and only Brent and Lambeth councils provide Afro-Caribbean meals). Certainly the delicious cooking smells which abound in these centres near lunch-time add very agreeably to the atmosphere. Some Asian clubs also prepare their own food or would like to do so (nos 2,7,9,11,12,15) and in almost all cases this is vegetarian as being most generally acceptable, though Muslims may find a meatless diet inadequate. The Cypriot club in Haringey would also prefer this solution (no 29). Careful consideration therefore needs to be given to providing assistance with cooking and catering on the premises when considering the funding of a new centre. Nottinghamshire, in particular, has made such provision part of its policy of supporting specialist lunch clubs, and it also provides transport to take housebound people to these centres instead of taking meals to their homes where they would have to eat alone.

One alternative to preparing food on the spot is to buy in from a suitable local restaurant. Leicestershire has a scheme by which a Section 11-funded social worker assesses Asian applicants for the service and arranges for meals to be obtained from an appropriate restaurant and delivered by a driver with Asian language skills. However, it is hoped that the Scope kitchen will soon be able to meet a considerable proportion of the need (no 1).

In general, buying-in from restaurants does not seem to be a very satisfactory solution for any large scale provision: restaurateurs are usually reluctant to make any mass-produced dish to suit individual medical needs and costs are usually high. Also the Food Hygiene Regulations covering eating places are less stringent, and their observance less carefully monitored, than those applying to factories which produce prepared food. Any local authority has a duty to its clients to see that food distributed to them has been prepared in such a way that there is no danger of food poisoning. There may also be problems with collection and delivery in council-owned vehicles, because trades unions object to what they see as 'privatisation'.

The third possibility is to buy in meals from an established specialist bulk supplier. Thus Lambeth buys in frozen kosher meals from the London Hospital's Kosher Meals Service and distributes them to Jewish clients on a daily basis in exactly the same way as it provides for the gentile population. It also charges the same subsidised price, although the kosher meals are more expensive. This unique service is well-used and much appreciated. Less highly regarded are the frozen 'Asian' meals sold to Haringey and Lambeth by Islington's highly sophisticated centralised kitchens. These have been variously described to the author as 'really being Bengali food and not acceptable to other groups', 'all tasting the same' and 'not being really Asian' and they certainly attract few takers in Lambeth or Haringey. A local authority may also co-operate with a voluntary organisation to provide an acceptable service. For example, Brent subsidises the cost of meals prepared for the Jewish Welfare Board in the Stanmore Synagogue in Harrow and distributed by Jewish volunteers (it is now planning to provide kosher meals itself). Whatever the source of supply, buying in of prepared food has its disadvantages because the purchaser cannot control quality and ensure acceptability and because it is difficult or impossible to cater for special individual diets—diabetic, low fat, low salt, high fibre or high protein, for example.

Finally, a local authority can decide to set up its own specialist meals services catering for one or more of the communities in its area. This needs to be done with great care to ensure that ritual and other requirements are carried out to the full satisfaction of the community concerned and that standards are not only set but maintained. This is not always achieved. Lambeth, for example, established a successful Afro-Caribbean service using a white cook trained by the catering manager's assistant who was of Afro-Caribbean origin. This assistant has now left the job, however, and without specialist supervision the meals produced are becoming more European in style and less acceptable. Birmingham has also attempted to set up its own Asian meals, but has not employed an Asian cook and there is said to be deep suspicion as to whether the food is really being correctly prepared. Certainly take-up has been extremely small.

As has been noted several times in this report, Brent has had most success in providing its own acceptable Asian vegetarian meals service. The demand for this was recognised as early as 1975 when Brent Social Services Department was receiving a small but constant trickle of referrals for meals-on-wheels from housebound elderly Asian people, and the Brent Asian Elders Group (no. 5) also wished to run a lunch club for their elderly members. A great deal of discussion took place between Brent and BAEG about the nature of the Asian meals required, and in August 1975 a council meals service was set up which used Asian staff employed by the council and was fully integrated with the mainstream meals services. This now goes to six community-based clubs, but it also goes to Asian clients in local authority day centres and to housebound people. The quality of the service is monitored by an Asian food committee comprising representatives from the clubs who talk with Brent about the brass tacks of provision. Funding was originally from urban aid. This was necessary to get things going, but was against the wishes of the meals co-ordinator who felt strongly that such a basic service should be funded from mainstream sources, and this is now being done. She also feels that it is wrong in principle for social services departments to shirk their responsibilities by farming out a basic service to voluntary groups on the pretext that they do not have the necessary expertise to run it when, as she has certainly proved, it is perfectly possible to do so, given the right attitude and resources.

All these forms of provision can only meet the needs of the larger ethnic communities whose numbers justify the cost of a specialist service. For the very many members of smaller groups the only acceptable solution is to recruit someone from the client's own community to provide cooked meals. This works well in Coventry, for example, where the Good Neighbour Scheme, which was formerly used to supplement the ordinary meals service, recruits people locally to help with specialist meals. Applicants are assessed by a domiciliary care organiser who is herself Asian and both clients and 'good neighbours' are recruited through a multi-language leaflet and through visits to community organisations. This type of 'bought in' specialist care should always be available to the social worker or domiciliary care organiser as a possible option when circumstances justify its use.

As with many other points made in this report, what is said about good service provision for ethnic groups applies with equal force to the indigenous community. Food which is unacceptable in quality, variety, or suitability in catering for special diets and tastes is all too common whether in meals-on-wheels services, lunch clubs, hospitals or residential homes. Better provision for ethnic minority elders must go hand in hand with stronger determination to provide all elderly people who cannot cater for themselves with meals which are both nourishing and enjoyable.

Information and advice services
The previous section suggested that acceptable provision of specialist meals was basic to many other services. The same can be said of access to competent and trustworthy sources of information, advice and counselling. This is not a need which is confined to elderly people or to any particular ethnic group. Study after study has shown that lack of accessible information about welfare rights is a problem common to the population as a whole. However, elderly immigrants have grown up in a country with a completely different social system. In addition they have to cope with language and cultural barriers and racist attitudes, and may have difficulty in providing the documentation needed to prove their entitlement to benefit. It can be impossible for them to make their way through the welfare rights jungle without assistance. It is not only welfare rights which create problems, however. As we have already seen, breakdown in family life, acute housing problems, difficulty in communicating with health service and other professionals, personal isolation, and despair can all give rise to situations in which skilled help and support is needed. Often a community will try to meet such needs from within its own resources. The unpublished Social Work Service (SWS) study quoted in Chapter 2, (p. 32) for instance, reported that:

'One of the most significant of the project's findings was the extent to which the local Asian community responded to its own diverse

108

social problems. Many of these problems, if occurring in the white population, would have been appropriately referred to and assisted by statutory services, including the District Team. Even though the sources of help used often produced only a 'rough and ready' assistance, they were on balance preferred to agencies outside the community which were judged to be insensitive and lacking in understanding of many of the elements of complex family and social relationships.

There was no Asian agency as such (available) to deal specifically with personal problems, but a number of organisations—mainly religious or cultural—had taken on the task. Several of these visited during the project were obviously well aware of the distress generated by matrimonial conflict, the isolation of the elderly and inter-generational differences. Their methods of responding to such problems might be totally ad hoc or more systematic, depending partly upon the strength and size of the organisation.

Obviously not all —— Asians were drawn in times of trouble to their nominal faith. Some saw religious organisations as rigid or disliked the risk of exposing personal difficulties to a wider audience. But a significant number of leaders did respond to a wide variety of problems presented by their congregations. One Muslim Imam indicated how he was used: "You should see my living-room on a Saturday morning. Many people come in very great personal trouble. My wife and I try to help them at least in some small way". . .

The other main source of help was a diverse group of local people, used sometimes because of their status as political or community leaders, but more often because of their social concern and literacy in English. This group of well-meaning key people was thought to respond even more extensively than religious organis-ations to a range of problems which were every bit as acute as those which social workers handled. In addition, they were used as advisers on welfare rights and other benefits and services. Some of those interviewed were conscious of their limited knowledge. One adviser, for instance, had made informal fostering arrange-ments at the request of a father whose wife was admitted to hospital. Neither the adviser nor the applicant were aware of the relevant social service provision.

A consistent finding by the project team was that both religious and secular helpers lacked knowledge of services which might have assisted those who turned to them for help. In consequence, few referrals were made to social services or other agencies outside the Asian community.'

This study confirms a point which was made repeatedly by people concerned with advice-giving, and that is that the adviser must be personally known to and trusted by the client. This is true for any age group, but particularly for elderly people. The manager of the Minorities Resource Centre in Saltley, Birmingham put it graphically when speaking of the local Muslim population, almost all of whom came from rural Pakistan: 'They will not ask for any help unless they know you personally—they have been cheated so often that they fear there is a catch in any offer of help—it is like a desperately thirsty man who sees water but is afraid to drink'. Other communities may have a less extreme attitude, but the basic need to know and trust the information giver remains valid and this is why clubs and centres are so important as sources of advice for older people from the minority communities. Again and again centre organisers emphasised to the author the importance of a personal relationship, a private but informal setting in which to talk, and a deep concern for the dignity of the person seeking help. As Mr G Ganatra of Scope Leicester put it, 'Every old man comes with his dignity. If we protect that dignity, we help him. If we do not protect it, the help is nothing.'

Thus, both centre organisers and other community leaders who are trusted to provide advice, information, interpretation and advocacy need access to knowledge and training which will enable them to be fully informed in their work. Varied means can be used to achieve this. There is, for example, growing realisation of the need for information on welfare rights and available services to be translated into appropriate languages and made fully available. This is not yet done nearly carefully and thoroughly enough, however. The SWS study quoted above found that:

'Communication was seen as a central issue and a priority need was for the development of schemes to facilitate information exchange and forge links between the (SSD) team and the local Asian people of —— Asian assistance was offered in the preparation of leaflets and other literature which, it was emphasised, should be made available in all Asian languages and in a form which was interesting and readily intelligible. Information should be posted throughout the area in public buildings, supplied to religious and social organisations and distributed to houses in streets known to contain large numbers of Asian families. Other agencies and professionals should be asked to co-operate in the wide dissemination of information about sources of help and in this respect, social services could make much greater use of health visitors who had the entree to many Asian homes.'

Written information by itself is not enough, however. It needs to be used and supplemented by personal visits to community groups of all kinds and to clubs and day centres for elderly people to talk about particular aspects of service provision. Such visits are usually welcome if they are properly arranged. To quote the SWS study again:

'It was suggested that social workers might initiate meetings and also obtain invitations to attend Asian groups belonging to the major religious, industrial and social organisations. These visits were thought to stand a good chance of success if workers went 'in a spirit of friendship and in a situation of non-crisis' to explain the concept of social services, the provisions offered and the opportunities for Asian people to assist. More detailed information about the role and tasks of the Department and other relevant public service agencies, together with training seminars on welfare rights and benefits should also be offered to the advisers and helpers who were being used by people in their neighbourhood. The venue of such courses could be the premises of the various organisations, both to facilitate attendance and as an expression of the Department's good will.'

One useful potential means of providing such information is much more extensive use of video tapes on appropriate subjects and in appropriate languages. This is surely a project on which education and training departments could usefully work with the communities concerned and with voluntary organisations. One such initiative is already being taken by the Asian Community Action Group (ACAG) in Lambeth which is negotiating with the Greater London Enterprise Board and the Greater London Council to obtain funding for a welfare rights video project. Tapes will be made in various languages and will be used as an educational resource with outlets throughout community groups, libraries, educational bodies and health clinics.[5] The Family Welfare Association is also planning a video tape intended to meet the specific needs of isolated Asian women.

Established voluntary advice agencies could also do much more to help in providing an information service to members of ethnic minorities, but the difficulties which have to be worked through are considerable. They have been well documented in a report by the National Association of Citizens Advice Bureaux (NACAB)[6] which describes an experimental attempt to make the CAB service more accessible to members of ethnic minority groups in the Kirklees district of West Yorkshire. This report should be read in full by all organisations, whether statutory or voluntary, which are concerned to 'sensitise' any kind of service provison. It spells out the need to support and act as a resource to existing advice networks rather than supplanting them. It enumerates the various reasons for confusion about and suspicion of the CAB role on the part of potential clients, and shows that fresh thinking is needed about recruiting and training processes if volunteers from the ethnic minorities and young unemployed people are to be successfully encouraged. It discusses the new styles of advice-giving which may be necessary and the conscious and unconscious racist attitudes in established bureaux which result in both volunteers and clients from the ethnic minorities feeling rejected and devalued; and much more besides. In spite of the difficulties which it documents, the report concludes that given sufficient determination to rethink procedures and practices which at present exclude ethnic minority involvement at management, worker, volunteer and client level, a great deal can be achieved, and it urges the NACAB Council to promote and support developments in this direction.

One important example of what *can* be done is provided by the Citizens Advice Bureau in Chapeltown, Leeds. This CAB was visited while undertaking the pilot field study for this report. It is based in a purpose-built building in the Methodist Church complex and employs a specialist paid staff (some from the ethnic minorities) to work respectively on consumer/debt counselling, housing, disability rights, and the compilation of information booklets on such subjects as the new nationality law. It also has four people working in a Tribunal Assistance Unit. This specialist unit provides training in social security appeals procedures for voluntary and statutory workers from all over the city, and deals with enquiries from all over the country.

In addition, there are two workers (both of Asian origin) who work particularly with the Asian community, and nearly forty trained volunteers offering at least three hours a week. Many of these are of West Indian or Asian origin. The Bureau also employs people on work experience courses. These have often missed out completely on formal education, but at least they have lived with the social security system and know what it is like to be dependent on it and they are keen to find out how it works. Some of these trainees are now working as volunteers and hope to go on to formal community work or welfare rights training. On a less ambitious scale, Brent Age Concern employs two advice workers, one of whom is a specialist in Asian languages and the other in services for disabled people. The main emphasis of their work is to provide a domiciliary advice service to housebound and disabled people, covering issues such as welfare rights, fuel and housing problems. Referrals are made in the main by the social services department, other advice agencies who cannot make home visits, GPs and the clients themselves who have gradually got to know of the service via the local newspapers, radio, the library service and word of mouth. Contact has been developed with various local community groups, and regular advice sessions are held in two neighbourhood centres. The workers have also talked about welfare rights and social services at neighbourhood classes for speakers of English as a second language, and feel that these visits have been particularly enjoyable and successful and have produced a marked improvement in take-up of benefits. Brent Age Concern has built up a fairly comprehensive information pack for older people with detailed information on local services, welfare benefits and such matters as the codes of practice of the fuel boards. This pack is being translated into Gujarati and it is hoped that it will go a long way towards alleviating the confusion and lack of knowledge about statutory provision of services and benefits.

It has not been possible within the scope of this study to undertake any review of the range of advice services funded by urban aid and designed to serve the needs of particular ethnic groups or residents in a particular locality. The number and variety of these is very considerable and the DoE study[7] suggests that there is a need for individual local authorities, in consultation with the voluntary agencies concerned, to start developing a local policy and strategy for advice provision which could combine resources and knowledge, give direction and priority, and minimise duplication without reducing the effectiveness of the services concerned.

Educational and library services
It was clear from the visits made in the course of preparing the chapter on clubs and day centres that there is a strong demand from these clubs for access to magazines, books and video films; help in improving literacy and language skills (both in English and the mother tongue), education about the history and culture of both England and the country of origin, and the opportunity to acquire

skills in dressmaking, cookery, music-making and many other subjects. All too often these demands are not met because of unsuitable
premises, lack of funding for teachers, lack of knowledge by the
club organisers of possible sources of help and a shortage of
the necessary materials and teaching skills. The adult education
authorities have indeed tried hard in some areas. In the Foleshill
area of Coventry, for example, the Community Education Development Centre has set up six centres, offering a range of classes to
Asian men and women and these are much appreciated. But much
more needs to be done to bring educational opportunities within
reach of *all* members of the ethnic minority communities who wish
to make use of them, and especially to bring them within reach of
older people who may need much help and encouragement to start
learning about the language and culture of the environment in
which they find themselves, and to realise that they themselves have
knowledge and skills which would benefit others. The concept of the
University of the Third Age has a great deal to offer in this regard in
its emphasis on the potential of older people both as teachers and
learners and the fineness of the line which divides education from
recreation. Its advocates emphasise that older people of any ethnic
background probably remember their early education (if they had
any formal education at all) as a dull, hard and frightening experience which they do not want to repeat.[8] Getting over this barrier
and helping older people to realise both the enjoyment and the use-
fulness of extending their horizons is an essential though difficult
task. It can be done, as the success of the clubs run by Ben Gamadia
in Leicester (no 10) and many other initiatives described in this
report indicate, and it is to be hoped that the Forum on the Rights
of Elderly People to Education (FREE) will continue to take a
serious and effective interest in this field.

It has not been possible within the time available for preparing this
report to take any detailed look at the provision of specialised education and library services. This could and should be the subject of a
study in its own right. However, this section does seek to illustrate
the sort of library service which is needed and what can be achieved
by describing briefly one initiative undertaken in the London
Borough of Wandsworth.

The Ethnic Minorities Library and Cultural Centre was opened in
Tooting library in 1977 with an urban aid grant. Initially it was
hoped to offer a library service and promote cultural activities to
all immigrant and foreign language speaking groups, but from
the start particular emphasis was given to those speaking Asian

languages and this was reinforced by the appointment of an Asian as librarian in charge and an Asian clerical assistant. Since then, the Centre's establishment has been increased to provide another Asian librarian, an Afro-Caribbean librarian, an ethnic minorities children's librarian and an ethnic minorities arts officer, and the available space and range of facilities have been greatly expanded. There is no doubt that there is much room for still further growth.

The senior librarian, Mrs Patel, is an East African Gujarati with a particular concern for elderly library users. She has built up a library stock in all the main Asian languages. This includes newspapers, periodicals (important sources of reading material which are loaned out like books and are very popular), novels (these are often in two or three volumes and it is important to make sure that they are kept together), books on spiritual and religious subjects which are very popular with older readers, tape cassette recordings of literature of all kinds (useful for those who are illiterate and for those who cannot read small print since largeprint books for adults in the Asian languages are virtually non existent), and cassettes of classical music and devotional music and reading, including 35 cassettes of the Koran. Cassette recordings also help to replace the traditional oral story-telling and preaching customary in less book-oriented cultures, and provide early morning hymn-singing which women would have taken part in while doing the household chores when in their home villages.

Older people are encouraged to make use of these resources by a friendly, informal atmosphere with space to sit and chat, and by Mrs Patel's success in establishing a personal relationship with borrowers. She gets to know the needs, tastes and capacities of each client and so can order new titles with a specific person in mind or send a supply of acceptable books to a branch library so that a reader who cannot get to Tooting frequently can obtain books locally. Her personal knowledge also enables her to select suitable books for housebound readers. Elderly people come from all over London to use the library with the help of the free bus pass, and others have relatives who bring them by car on Saturday—which means that it is important that Mrs Patel should herself be present on Saturdays. Her activities are by no means confined to the library, however, and she gets involved in a very wide range of community-based cultural activities, in teaching both students and tutors in English language classes, and in taking the library service to Asian clubs, day centres and sheltered housing. Even with the recent expansion in staff, there are not enough hours in her day and the demand for her services is some indication of the hunger for services of this kind if they are made available in a sensitive and caring way.

One important initiative in which the Wandsworth service has taken an active part has been the establishment of a scheme known as Co-operation of Indic Laser Library Authorities (CILLA). This organisation started in 1981 with five London library authorities and now has a membership of thirteen including some in the East Midlands. Books are bought co-operatively four times a year and catalogued by experts in each of the five major Indic languages. As a result of CILLA, higher standards of cataloguing are achieved and a much better service is now received from the book suppliers in this country. Almost all publications have to be imported and different suppliers deal in particular languages so that it is very important to maintain close contact with a number of them and not rely on one or two which cannot offer a sufficiently comprehensive service.

The Ethnic Minorities Library in Tooting is also working in the Afro-Caribbean field and, as was noted above, has a specialist librarian to cover this sector. Here, however, the service has been provided rather differently with strong emphasis on encouraging the local branches to build up their own stock of material on such subjects as Afro-Caribbean history, Rastafarianism, black beauty, black women and reggae. Books are sent on approval from specialist bookshops so that the Afro-Caribbean librarian and the branch librarians can make a joint selection. This ensures that the whole library service, including the mobile services and Wandsworth prison, are aware of the availability of this material. Twelve black periodicals are also bought and well-used, and a central reserve collection with 1,200 volumes and multiple copies of all titles is available to make bulk loans to local groups, institutions and others working with and for the black community. This is in addition to an exhibition collection which is a single copy collection representing the wide range of black literature available in this country and is used by local schools, colleges and community centres for educational, cultural and display purposes.

The Afro-Caribbean service, like the Asian service, puts a lot of emphasis on outreach work, involvement in cultural activities and the use of libraries to provide information and advice on a wide range of subjects. Indeed, even in the non-specialist services the dividing line between a library service and an information and advice service seems to be becoming increasingly hard to distinguish not only in the personal welfare field but also in relation to the provision of information for businesses, and for counselling agencies which deal with subjects like legal and consumer problems, housing, social security and finance. For older settlers, another potentially important expansion of library activities is in encouraging groups to make 'living history' tape recordings of their experiences and memories. Such tapes are urgently needed to provide a record of a unique generation whose experience will never be repeated, and they can be invaluable in enabling younger people from the same community to understand their cultural roots and in informing members of other communities about the experience. It is very much to be hoped that librarians will put increasing effort into working with education authorities, day centres and clubs to create and disseminate tapes and shared writing of this kind.

Similar close co-operation is needed in encouraging the teaching of English. As was noted in Leicester, older women are very anxious to learn English so that they can move about more freely and communicate with their neighbours, and indeed with their own grandchildren (no 10). It is much easier for them to embark on this challenging task if the teacher is of the same sex and comes from the same culture. Even if this results in the English which is taught being less formally correct, it gives much greater confidence, as explanations can be given first in the learner's own language. Also if the teacher understands the thinking and culture of her pupils, she can interpret English ways of thinking and behaving to them. There is, therefore, a serious need in all the groups where English is not the first language that English-speaking members of the community be trained in basic teaching techniques so that they can work in co-operation with the libraries and education authorities to bring learning opportunities within reach of older settlers. There is also a considerable demand from older women for literacy teaching both in English and the mother tongue and opportunities for this should be made much more widely available.

This brief discussion is at least enough to indicate the immense scope for development in the provision of education and library services. Section 11 money (see p. 140) is available for this purpose, but funding alone is not enough. Real concern, sensitivity and enthusiasm on the part of the specialist workers and real support and encouragement by colleagues and senior staff are needed if educational opportunity and access to library facilities are to become a reality for all those older members of ethnic minority groups who would like to make use of them.

Conclusion

This chapter illustrates both the complexity and the potential value of 'sensitising' local authority services and integrating them with community-based, voluntary provision. It *is* possible to support voluntary initiatives in domiciliary service provision, widen recruitment to the statutory services and work out policies for appropriate deployment. It *is* possible to provide specialist meals for the main ethnic minority communities from local authority kitchens in an acceptable way and to distribute them to clubs, hospitals, day centres and residential homes, and it is also possible to make imaginative use of cooking facilities in specialist day centres, to buy in from restaurants and to recruit neighbours to cook for housebound people on a one-to-one basis. It *is* possible to improve the accessibility of the information and advice services provided by local authorities and Citizens Advice Bureaux through reviewing recruitment policy, translating leaflets, and providing a resource to existing advice networks, though this needs to be combined with funding and supporting the advice-giving role of workers in clubs and day centres. It *is* possible to develop educational and library services, so that they really do meet the needs of older members of ethnic minority groups.

The potential is almost limitless, but the actuality is still very limited. All these areas of service provision demand urgent and detailed consideration.

SUMMARY OF ACTION REQUIRED

Action by ethnic minority groups
1. Publicise the availability of the home help service and encourage its use by those who need it.
2. Press the local authority to recruit home helps in a way which encourages members of ethnic minority groups to apply for jobs.
3. Develop specialist voluntary domiciliary support schemes to supplement home helps and provide an acceptable service to those who cannot use the home help service.
4. Press for correctly prepared and acceptable meals to be made available through hospital and local authority catering services.
5. Press for recruitment of 'good neighbours' by the local authority to cook for and look after housebound people for whom appropriate local authority home help and meals-on-wheels cannot be made available.

6. Ensure that informal advice and counselling services have access to information about welfare rights and local authority services, and liaise with local authorities to achieve this.

7. Work with local authorities and organisations, such as Citizens Advice Bureaux, to translate welfare rights information and local information clearly and accurately, and ensure that the resulting literature is widely publicised and distributed.

8. Invite experts on particular topics to talk to community groups, clubs and day centres.

9. Obtain relevant video tapes on health education, welfare rights, etc and show them in clubs and day centres.

10. Encourage unemployed or retired members of ethnic minority groups to volunteer for work in information agencies such as Citizen Advice Bureaux and Age Concern offices.

11. Press for the provision of really accessible and appropriate library and adult education services.

12. Encourage members of ethnic minority groups, and especially older women who can speak English, to assist in language classes for older people.

13. Encourage the recording of 'living history' based on the experiences of older people.

Action by local authorities

1. Publicise the availability of domiciliary support services and offer talks on the subject in clubs and day centres.

2. Review home help recruitment procedures and establish a system which encourages applications from members of ethnic minority groups at both worker and organiser levels.

3. Consider funding specialist voluntary domiciliary services or appointing home helps specifically to work with a particular community, when this is desired and appropriate.

4. Think carefully through the issues which may arise when deploying home helps to work for people from a different culture, including meeting training needs and matching client to helper.

5. Review and make appropriate arrangements to meet the demand for specialist meals services, taking care to consult with representatives from the communities concerned and to ensure that the quality of meals is regularly monitored by such representatives.

6. Make appropriate individual arrangements to meet the dietary and other needs of housebound people for whom the meals provided for the main ethnic group are not appropriate.

7. Review and, if necessary, improve the quality, acceptability and range of choice available in the *basic* meals service.
8. Offer appropriate support and assistance to informal and voluntary information and advice services, including those run in conjunction with clubs and day centres.
9. Work with representatives of the ethnic minority groups on the preparation of information leaflets about welfare rights and local services and facilities.
10. Develop specialist library facilities which are sensitive to the particular needs of older people, and encourage outreach work by librarians to clubs and day centres, as well as to individuals and adult education classes.
11. Encourage the involvement of specialist librarians in cultural and educational activities, and in the creation of 'living history'.
12. Make available language and other teaching to older adults, making extensive use of potential teachers within the community concerned with particular emphasis on finding appropriate means of meeting the educational needs of older women.

Action by traditional voluntary organisations
1. Recruit volunteer visitors and 'good neighbours' from members of ethnic minority groups and work through the issues which arise in using volunteers to befriend a person from a different culture.
2. If involved in meals-on-wheels delivery, consider the needs of potential clients from the ethnic minority groups and urge the local authority to see that they are appropriately met.
3. If involved in selling basic foodstuffs to pensioners at wholesale prices, make sure that foods used by members of ethnic minority groups are also available and that suitably sited and staffed points of sale are established.
4. Make advisory services more accessible to members of ethnic minority groups by tackling racist attitudes in volunteers, staff, management and clients and by making a positive effort to recruit volunteers and staff from ethnic minority groups.
5. Build up contact with advice and counselling agencies run by ethnic minority groups and offer appropriate support and back-up services.
6. Work with ethnic minority groups on the production of trans-lated information packs and leaflets in appropriate languages.
7. Offer talks on welfare rights and social services provision to clubs, day centres and language classes.

120

8. Be informed about the provision of specialist library and educational facilities in the area and help in publicising these and encouraging their use.

REFERENCES
1. Anil Bhalla and Ken Blakemore, *Elders of the ethnic minority groups*, AFFOR, Birmingham, 1981.
2. Stewart Berry, Mike Lee and Sue Griffiths, *Report on a survey of West Indian pensioners in Nottingham*, Nottinghamshire County Council Social Services Department, Research Section, January 1981.
3. J M Cooper, *Elderly West Indians in Leicester*, unpublished MA in Social Service Planning, University of Essex Department of Sociology, 1976.
4. Alix Henley and Jim Clayton, Catering for all tastes, *Health and Social Service Journal*, 22 July 1982, pp 888–9.
5. Asian Community Action Group, Lambeth, *Annual Report*, London, 1983.
6. The Kirklees Ethnic Minorities Advice Project, *Final Report*, CAB occasional paper 16, National Association of Citizens Advice Bureaux, London 1984.
7. Stuart Elliott, Graham Lomas, Alan Riddell, *Community Projects Review; a review of voluntary projects receiving Urban Programme funding*, Department of the Environment, London, 1984.
8. Eric Midwinter, *Age is opportunity: education and older people*, Centre for Policy on Ageing, London, 1982.

7 'Umbrella' organisations

Introduction

Much of this report has been concerned with self-help initiatives taken by the ethnic minority communities themselves on behalf of their elderly members and the relationship between these initiatives and statutory provision. It is, however, important to emphasise that these projects have developed alongside a massive, long-established, voluntary sector which has, as yet, done little to recognise that we are living in a multi-cultural society—whether in employment policy, staff and volunteer training, committee membership, relationships with ethnic minority voluntary organisations or provision of services to individuals in the minority groups. One important step forward has now been taken by the National Council for Voluntary Organisations (NCVO) through its recent publication, *A multi-racial society: the role of national voluntary organisations.*[1] This report describes the findings of a questionnaire sent to 194 organisations within NCVO's Health and Handicaps and Personal and Family Services interest groups asking about their policy as employers and as service providers in relation to the minority groups. The response indicated that national organisations have little information about the activities of their constituent local branches and that there is a general lack of any coherent policy in this field.

The report goes on to discuss the implications of being an equal opportunities employer, making services accessible and developing genuine partnership with ethnic minority voluntary organisations. It is seen by NCVO as the beginning of a consistent effort to get the 'ethnic dimension' accepted as a built-in element of all voluntary activity which is not specifically directed towards members of a particular community.

There is a tremendous amount to be done, both in opening up established services for use by members of minority communities and in offering resources and support to minority organisations which would like to make use of such help. The sort of help which would be acceptable to and accepted by many 'black' minority organisations was detailed by Dr Vince Hines of the National Federation of Self-Help Organisations at the conference which NCVO called to launch its report.

He suggested that it might include:
offers to share resources, including use of premises and committee rooms, equipment, teaching aids, transport and secretarial facilities;

exercises in joint fund-raising;

use of established credibility to encourage grant-givers to assist ethnic minority initiatives;

regular consultation to establish good routine working relationships at local, regional and national level;

the promotion of representation of the black sector at meetings with the statutory authorities and, where this has not been achieved, ascertaining what policies black organisations want to have put forward and making these known;

direct approaches to black groups for their views rather than relying on an intermediary 'race relations adviser' (such reliance, Dr Hines suggested, was like two English-speaking people talking to each other through an interpreter);

appointment of committee members from the black population;

encouragement to black groups to share in training programmes.

Initiatives by organisations concerned with the care of elderly people
Age Concern England (ACE) is trying to develop positive policies in this field and encourage its constituent organisations to take them up. As we have seen, it has undertaken some original research into the life experience and social situations of Afro-Caribbean and Asian elders[2] and it has begun to provide training courses for workers interested in this field. ACE is now developing a strategy which will include a review of its own employment practices, publications policy, press releases and so on with a view to eliminating racial bias, promoting the needs and rights of the ethnic elderly, and encouraging much greater awareness of the 'ethnic' dimension among its local groups.

Some examples of successful co-operation or 'sensitising' of service provision at local level came to light in the course of preparing this report. It has already been noted that Brent Age Concern provides peripatetic advisers on welfare rights and services for disabled people in their own homes (see p. 112). This organisation also puts a lot of effort into supporting and co-operating with specialist voluntary organisations in their fight through the funding jungle.

Lambeth Age Concern has also worked hard to make contact with local groups and sought their advice and help on the inclusion of Afro-Caribbean and Asian foods in the cost-price groceries which Lambeth Age Concern sells to pensioners. Suitable outlets for these sales have been opened up in the places where ethnic minority elders congregate and volunteers have been recruited from the communities to help sell the goods. This in turn has involved working with European volunteers on their attitudes to members of other communities and improving their knowledge about how the ethnic foodstuffs are grown and used. Just one initiative has therefore opened up a whole range of opportunities for training, education, consultation and recruitment. Taking a different approach, Age Concern Leicester has, as we have seen, succeeded in launching several specialist initiatives using an Asian worker (no 10 in Appendix 1). And on a regional level, Age Concern Greater London (ACGL) employs a development officer to work with ethnic minorities organisations, raise awareness of the needs of the ethnic elderly and encourage more informed discussion about how those needs can be met. This development officer helped to establish the Conference of Ethnic Minority Senior Citizens which provides a forum in which the many specialist organisations in the London area can discuss their common needs and interests and call public attention to them; the conference now has two paid staff and its own premises paid for by GLC funding.

Initiatives such as these are unfortunately as yet only a drop in the ocean. When ACE sent a questionnaire on the subject to 104 major groups only 13 replied, while in the London area nine out of fifty responded to an ACGL enquiry. The ethnic minority development officer responsible for organising the latter commented on 'the lack of commitment and enthusiasm generally evident' in this field. 'The typical reaction has been that elderly people in these communities must use the services provided.'

Pensioners Link (formerly Task Force) has always put much of its emphasis on encouraging self-help initiatives amongst pensioners and helping them to publicise and assert rights and needs so its workers are well placed to work with minority groups. In Hackney, for example, Pensioners Link has close contact with the HEADS club and has helped members to use non-segregated facilities (no 24) while in Haringey, Pensioners Link workers have enabled two Afro-Caribbean clubs to get off the ground, both of which are based in ordinary community centres. One of these is specifically for disabled and housebound people and is organised jointly with

Tottenham Old People's Welfare Council who also supply transport. This Pensioners Link has a team of three staff which include an Asian fieldworker and an Afro-Caribbean worker (both funded through the Ethnic Minorities Unit of the GLC). Funds are being sought to employ a Cypriot worker as well, so as to be able to respond effectively to all the main sections of the Haringey community.

Initiatives by 'intermediary' organisations

Age Concern and Pensioners Link are specifically concerned with services to older people, but intermediary organisations such as councils of voluntary service, volunteer bureaux and community relations councils can provide a more general resource. Their potential role in monitoring the allocation of Urban Programme money and working with voluntary organisations and the local authority to achieve an agreed policy on priorities is particularly important. Birmingham Voluntary Service Council's Grant Aid Review Committee is one example of a serious attempt in this direction[3], as is a discussion paper by Leeds Community Relations Council on ethnic minorities and the Urban Programme in Leeds[4]. All too often, however, attempts of this kind are hamstrung by conflict. The traditional umbrella organisations are often reluctant to try to establish relationships with ethnic minority organisations, while the black ethnic minority groups are often deeply suspicious of organisations which may be seen as a potential threat to their independence and status as black people working on behalf of black people. Such antagonisms and suspicion also exist in some cases between one ethnic group and another. In Brent, for example, the local Voluntary Service Council failed completely to obtain a co-operative approach to policy on the allocation of Urban Programme funding and the Afro-Caribbean and Asian groups each set up their own 'umbrella' organisation to represent their own views and interests to the Council.

Initiatives by organisations providing a particular service

Yet another kind of 'umbrella' body is that which provides a service across the age groups to meet the needs of people with a particular illness or disability or provide a particular kind of service. Citizens Advice Bureaux, victim support schemes, arthritis care associations, mental health associations (MIND) and organisations which provide services for blind and deaf people are obvious examples with particular relevance for elderly people. There is no doubt that such organisations are not usually reaching potential clients in the ethnic minority communities and this is a situation which they need to address as a matter of urgency. Ways of doing this and examples of successful practice are outlined in the NCVO report.

The Multi-faith Resource Unit

It is worthwhile drawing attention to an initiative in Birmingham which has much potential for imitation elsewhere. This is the Multi-faith Resource Unit (MUFRU) in Birmingham, whose primary aim is to 'provide a space and opportunity for people from different religious backgrounds and cultures to work at understanding each others' beliefs, theology and traditions in relation to what they share together'. It started as a three-year research project sponsored by the Roman Catholic Bishops' Conference of England and Wales, and undertaken by Dr Mary Hall, a Roman Catholic nun. She persuaded members of 14 different religious denominations, representing Hindu, Muslim, Sikh, Buddhist, Jewish and Christian communities to meet together on a regular basis and explain to each other the nature and practice of their faith. It was found that this exercise made deep demands on participants who, in the process of trying to explain their beliefs to others, often found that they had to do a great deal of work in improving their own understanding. Over the three years, 156 people participated in these group meetings; mutual trust and comprehension developed at a really deep level and small groups of members often joined forces to explain their differing beliefs to an outside body. The groups were very anxious that the work should continue when the experimental period came to an end; funds were raised from charitable trusts to obtain premises and pay secretarial costs and the Multi-Faith Resource Centre opened in January 1982. Since then, it has worked in many different ways to improve relations between the various ethnic groups by enhancing their knowledge of one another.

Its teaching programme includes a 'Certificate in Religions'—a five-term evening programme carried out in co-operation with the Extramural Department of Birmingham University, with two religions being studied each term: Hinduism and Judaism; Sikhism and Christianity; Buddhism and Islam. In the first year 38 students from these communities attended these courses, which include lectures, seminars, discussions, visits and exercises to analyse the problems encountered in a multi-faith society. Study days are also set up to provide an opportunity for various groups to meet with members of other religions; lectures are given by members of the Multi-Faith team to organisations such as the Quaker Adult School; and numerous other teaching engagements include leading school assemblies followed by teaching sessions with the children. Other activities include radio and television presentations, response to student enquiries and the celebration of festivals and feasts. A research programme has also been initiated which will explore the current situation of Hindu, Muslim and Sikh communities in Birmingham, including the process of adaptation, the identification of group problems, evolving links with other communities, and priorities for the future. The three researchers are all members of MUFRU and each is a member of one of the faiths concerned. Other groups are now asking to join MUFRU and these are affiliated after undergoing the same initial training in sharing and self-understanding as was undertaken by the original members.

A half-hour ITV documentary film on the work of the unit called 'No one is trying to convert anyone' attracted requests to participate in training sessions from all over the country. A weekend crash course was arranged to demonstrate the sharing technique. Participants then went home to continue with the process they had been shown. A reunion, at which their subsequent experience can be shared, is planned. In essence, MUFRU offers both a learning resource and an opportunity for those who share the experience of living by religious faith in a largely agnostic or atheist world to recognise and rejoice in this basic common bond. This development shows what *can* be done to transcend barriers of race, language and belief, and every city with a mixed-race population should surely have its own Multi-Faith Resource Unit—though it will unfortunately prove difficult to provide them all with leaders of the calibre of Mary Hall.

Conclusion
This short chapter has not been able to begin to do justice to the importance or the complexity of established umbrella organisations taking on an appropriate 'ethnic dimension'. There are many issues to be worked out and much to be learned about the process of transition, especially when local groups may be extremely unwilling to follow a lead set by the centre. It is clearly a matter to be tackled seriously in many ways and at many levels if the services provided by these organisations are to be genuinely available to all who need them.

SUMMARY OF ACTION REQUIRED

Action by ethnic minority groups
1. Take the initiative in approaching relevant organisations and talking about ways in which co-operation could be established.

(Many traditional organisations are afraid of causing offence or being thought to be planning a takeover if they make the first approach.)
2. Put forward candidates for membership of management committees of umbrella organisations.
3. Find out about and use facilities relating to accountancy, publicity, publications, grant applications etc. which may be available to voluntary organisations in a particular locality.
4. Encourage individuals to make use of organisations providing particular kinds of support and care, and if they do not feel they have received a satisfactory service bring the matter to the organisation's attention.

Action by umbrella organisations
1. Review recruitment, and employment and training policy at committee, employee and volunteer level with a view to providing equal opportunities as an employer and accessible services as a service provider.
2. Consult with relevant ethnic minority voluntary bodies about the possibility of mutual co-operation and support.
3. Research the particular needs of older members of ethnic minority groups in relation to the objectives of the organisation and take appropriate action to meet them.
4. Work towards a common strategy agreed by all ethnic groups in relation to the local authority and its dealings with voluntary organisations.

Action by religious organisations
1. Make a positive attempt to find out about and understand the beliefs, theology, and traditions of members of other faiths.
2. Work towards the development of groups in which each individual explains his beliefs to others.
3. Work towards the increase of understanding and awareness and reduced racial prejudice in the congregation concerned.
4. Ensure that members of the congregation who belong to an ethnic minority group are warmly welcomed and made to feel at home.

REFERENCES
1. Michaela Dungate, *A multi-racial society: the role of national voluntary organisations*, Bedford Square Press/NCVO, London, 1984.
2. Jonathan Barker, *Black and Asian old people in Britain: first report of a research study*. Age Concern Research Unit, Mitcham, 1984.

3. Birmingham Voluntary Service Council Grant Aid Review Committee, *Final Report,* Birmingham, 1983.

4. John Roberts, *Ethnic minorities and the Urban Programme in Leeds—a discussion paper.* Leeds Community Relations Council, February 1984. Unpublished.

8 Funding issues

Introduction

Funding is obviously a key element in the development of any specialised services for older members of minority communities. Where should the money come from? On what criteria should it be provided? How should its use be monitored and controlled? At present, no authority is addressing these questions in any systematic or ordered kind of way and the whole grant-giving scene is becoming more confused and inequitable by the minute.

At one end of the scale of opinion about who should pay for what are those who state that the 'minority' communities are in fact in the majority in some inner city areas. They are ratepayers and citizens and their elderly members have a right to appropriate services paid for from the local authority budget and provided at the same level as those offered to the indigenous community. From this point of view, the use of *all* specialist sources of funding, whether Section 11 of the Local Government Act 1966, the Urban Programme, the Manpower Services Commission, Opportunities for Volunteering, the metropolitan counties 2p rate or anything else is essentially unjust. Basic services, it is argued, are not provided for the indigenous population from these sources and those for the ethnic minority communities should not be either. At the other extreme, there are those who argue that it is wrong to use public money to pay for specialist services to meet the tastes and needs of particular groups, and that if communities want such services they should provide them for themselves as the Jews have done. Whatever the theoretical standpoint, however, what happens in practice is that money for voluntary organisations providing specialist services comes from a mishmash of sources with no clear policy and no future security and is often not sufficient to provide a decent service in terms of either accommodation or staffing. Also, as will be discussed further below, ratecapping is beginning to bite, the GLC and the metropolitan counties are likely to go out of business and the Urban Programme is being increasingly directed to short-term capital projects in the economic sector, so that funding for voluntary work within the ethnic minority communities is going to become harder and harder to obtain.

The Urban Programme and ethnic minorities

Most of the projects described in the fourth chapter of this report receive a substantial part of their capital and revenue funding from the Urban Programme. As Appendix 3 explains, the Programme was set up in 1969 to provide a special source of financial aid to innovative projects designed to improve the environment and the economy and raise the quality of life in the inner cities. All applications have to be approved and forwarded by the local authority to central government, originally at the Home Office and now at the Department of the Environment (DoE). Central government pays 75 per cent of the cost of approved applications through the Urban Programme grant, the local authority carrying the rest. Local authorities have been able to use this money to finance their own inner city projects or to support voluntary or commercial initiatives, but government guidelines now give priority to industrial and commercial ventures requiring a one-off injection of capital and little or no revenue funding. Projects which provide services are therefore losing out. There has been general encouragement to use Urban Programme money to improve the lot of the ethnic minorities, as the report by the School for Advanced Urban Studies, *Ethnic minorities and the Urban Programme* explains:[1]

'Within this general framework of inner cities policy, it is possible to identify a number of policy statements over recent years which have referred to the needs of ethnic minorities. For example, the Inner Cities White Paper stated:

"Where members of the ethnic minorities in inner areas suffer the kinds of disadvantage experienced by all those who live there, they should benefit directly through measures taken to improve conditions, for example, in housing, education and jobs. In addition, the government intend to ensure that their particular needs are fully taken into account in the planning and implementation of policies for the inner areas and in the allocation of resources under the enlarged Urban Programme".

Again, the review of the traditional Urban Programme concluded:

"Assisting ethnic minorities has been an implicit objective of the Urban Programme since its inception. However, it is only since 1974 (Circular 11) that this aspect has been consistently and explicitly publicised. Two types of project may be said to be meeting this objective: schemes which are aimed directly at ethnic minorities and others which are directed at a wider group but have a high proportion of ethnic minorities among their clients".

The Department of the Environment continued to stress the ethnic component in partnership activity through their 1981 guidelines:—

"Due priority should also be given to projects designed to benefit disadvantaged minorities such as certain ethnic groups, particularly through the provision of work and training."

The Home Affairs Select Committee's report dealt explicitly with the Urban Programme:—

"The Urban Programme should remain the major source of finance for voluntary sector schemes designed to combat racial disadvantage. The Department should be more flexible in their attitude to long-term funding of projects."

As did the government's response—

"The Government's Urban programme is of particular benefit to the ethnic minorities, not only as a result of the projects designed to help them specifically, but also because nearly 40 per cent of the ethnic minorities live in partnership or programme authority areas."

The role of the Urban Programme in particular and of inner cities policy in general in relation to ethnic minorities has most recently, in February 1982, been emphasised by DoE ministers in response to the report of the Home Affairs Committee:—

"A number of authorities have used the preparation of an inner area programme as the focus for their development of policies and structures with regard to racial questions generally. We believe that this is a useful approach which an include wide consultation on applications for Urban Programme funding as well as discussion of broader issues".'

However, no two authorities go about this task in the same way and there is no requirement on them to provide a clear policy statement, either on the 'ethnic dimension' of the programme they put forward for funding or on their attitude to the voluntary sector. Certainly the allocation to ethnic minority projects does not always reflect their numbers. For instance, a recent DoE study of the Urban Programme in Birmingham and Hammersmith and Fulham[2] found that in Birmingham by 1983/84:

'... only 6·5 per cent of main programme grant was going on ethnic minority projects which has to be seen in the context of an inner city where the proportion of the whole population that is in households where the head was New Commonwealth born now stands at 43 per cent'.

Overall, however, the percentage of Urban Programme funds devoted to ethnic projects has risen steadily in the last five years and it is estimated that it will be 8·6 per cent in 1984/85. In money terms, the increase has been substantial since the total value of Urban Programme grants has risen from £202m in 1980/81 to an estimated £348m in 1984/85, of which £30m will go to ethnic projects.[3]

Setting priorities in the use of Urban Programme funds
There is much criticism, both in the literature and on the ground, of lack of clearly-stated policy in relation to the encouragement of bids and the selection of projects for recommendation to the Department of the Environment. Thus, the DoE study suggests:

'The vagueness of the consultation procedures, the open-ended nature of the bidding process, the generality of the guidelines and the lack of explicit criteria inevitably leads to a situation of "hit and miss" . . . If a strategy was agreed that identified certain groups who needed assistance such as black youth, the elderly, depressed women, parents of mentally and physically handicapped children, then the pressures on the local authority and individual politicians would be eased as they would be able to give clear reasons for the Council's priorities . . .

Other factors that would form a strategy would be an evaluation of the needs of a certain group based on such criteria as unemployment, knowledge of English, suffering greatest racial prejudice etc—such groups as the Vietnamese, the Bengalis and black youth would then be identified as needing support.

A strategic approach based on some criteria may also identify other issues that would mean that limited Urban Programme resources could be more effectively spent—for example, an analysis of youth provision in Leeds 4 and 6 may indicate that provision for ethnic minority youth as a whole may be more beneficial than funding a particular group for a community centre . . . '

Even if the local authority has worked out an agreed and consistent approach, it does not of course follow that central government will accept what is offered, since government priorities may be different.

This can be a cause of resentment and suspicion on the part of organisations which have lost out and which may not believe that the local authority has in fact recommended them. On the other hand, the loss of control to central government may enable the authority to push politically unpopular projects favouring ethnic minorities or inner city areas and then put the blame on the DoE. Administrative delays caused by central control or administrative ineptitude can cause major difficulties. For example, in February 1984, when control of Brent Council switched from Labour to Conservative, the DoE held up decisions on applications which had been put forward from the reserve list 'until the political situation had stabilised' and approval which should have been given in three months had not been received in six, although the money was supposed to be *spent* by the applicant by the end of March.

The squeeze on Urban Programme funding
Until recently, the Urban Programme has been a substantial and reasonably accessible source of supply for those who knew how to work the system, but this is no longer the case. One reason for this, as was noted above, is that policy in allocating grants has shifted to favour economic regeneration and environmental improvement with a strong emphasis on capital spending and resistance to revenue commitments. Since voluntary projects which are essentially about service provision have no hope of being self-funding after an initial capital injection, they are bound to lose out under this policy. Further, any revenue grants run for a maximum of four years in Partnership and Programme authorities rather than the five years allowed under the traditional Urban Programme, and there is strong resistance to renewing them—the theory being that those which are 'time expired' and have proved their worth should be taken onto the local authority's mainstream funding programme. In 1984/85, the scale of time expiry will increase dramatically, since the five-year approvals given in 1979/80 and the three-year approvals given in 1981/82 will coincide. Even if the government permitted it, renewing funding for these projects would mean the Programme 'silting up' so that very few new initiatives could get off the ground, but taking them into local authority mainstream funding could well prove difficult or impossible at a time when statutory services are being cut back under threat of rate-capping, and local authority employees are being made redundant. There is, therefore, a very real danger that many good existing projects providing a fully-tested service will go under just at the point at which they are most needed. The DoE study of Birmingham and Hammersmith and Fulham[4] said:

'We gained a widespread impression of gloom and despondency in many voluntary organisations about the future prospect of funding, both for new developments and for existing projects. Given their almost universal commitment to, and belief in, the value of their activities this inevitably led to a sense of frustration at what they saw as an inconsistent and wasteful approach. In particular, although aware of the distinction between Urban Programme and main funding, people in the voluntary sector consider that if a project is worth setting up with public funds, it is not reasonable to close it down after a set period simply because the lapse of time, or an emphasis on capital projects, makes it ineligible for continued UP funding.'

The study does go on to indicate that the Department's bark has been worse than its bite in insisting on the promotion of capital versus revenue expenditure, and that almost all time-expired projects have hitherto either been re-approved or taken into main programmes. It is very uncertain whether this can continue, however. To take one example, the leader of Hammersmith and Fulham Council has written to all organisations funded by the Hammersmith and Fulham Inner Area Programme (HFIAP) in the following terms:[5]

'You will no doubt be aware of the very serious financial situation the council is facing next year. The amount of cash being made available by the government has been reduced once again, and the penalties for exceeding the government's expenditure target will be raised to an unprecedented level. In order to avoid these massive financial penalties, it is imperative that we keep our spending next year within the government's expenditure target.

The effects of these very harsh constraints on our grant aid programmes could be very significant indeed, and there is an extra problem to be taken into account when considering projects funded through HFIAP. As you may know, these schemes, for which the Government contributes 75 per cent of the cost, are approved by the Department of the Environment, usually on a five-year basis. Until now, we have managed for the most part to persuade the DoE to continue such projects after the expiry of the original term. However, the possibility of continuing this arrangement on any substantial basis must now be considered very remote. The consequences of this could be very significant. If we are not able to extend the life of projects, we shall have to consider absorbing their full cost into the council's main

135

programmes, and that means finding the 75 per cent funding presently provided by the government. Alternatively, if we cannot find this money without exceeding our target (and this must be a distinct possibility) we shall have no alternative but to consider ceasing financial support to some schemes. This state of affairs is not one that I look forward to. It must seem ironic to you, as it does to me, that the government has in the past encouraged us to make full use of the Inner Area Programme, when we are now being asked to absorb so much of its expenditure into our main programme—and, at the same time, reduce our main programme significantly.'

He goes on to give formal warning that it may be necessary to curtail severely or even withdraw funding for projects which are time-expired. The DoE study[6] calls this kind of situation with masterly understatement 'a serious dilemma of resource allocation' and goes on:

'We find the present situation with regard to revenue-funded voluntary projects unsatisfactory. It is fairly clear that in the initial growth of the Urban Programme, a good many voluntary sector revenue schemes were accepted by local authorities without sufficient thought for the revenue consequences on main programmes when Urban Programme funding ceased. The Department of the Environment must bear some responsibility for this, in that we feel it did not make it clear early enough just what its attitude would be on time-expiry. In fact, we do not feel even now that there is a clear policy. The guidelines are too vague, and in any case they are not matched by the practice, which seems to be that the Department has been prepared to refund any time-expired projects up to the limit of the revenue funds available. The result is that local authorities have been encouraged to put forward as many time-expired projects for refunding as possible, and to regard main programme funding as a fall-back position only to be used when refunding under the Urban Programme is not possible.

We ourselves are in no doubt that indefinite revenue funding under the Urban Programme is not desirable. Every scheme must reach a point where, on its own track record, it has either reached a sufficiently high place in the local authority's priorities to find a place in the main programme, or else it has to give way to something else. Space for new development must be maintained within the programme. We recognise that there are difficulties about the availability of main programme resources, and that some local authorities may be less ready than others to recognise that a voluntary sector project has established its claim to a place in the main programme. But we feel that the existing ad hoc arrangements, under which practice varies from one region to another and one year to the next, have contributed to the current difficulties.

We therefore recommend that a series of guidelines should be developed setting out in some detail the criteria for granting initial funding to voluntary sector projects under the Urban Programme, and the criteria for refunding at time-expiry. These guidelines should in part aim to ensure that proposals are considered in context—the aims of the Urban Programme, the priority attached to the need which they propose to meet, the extent to which the proposal will help meet the need, the continued funding requirement and so on. They should also relate to the effectiveness of the individual project, and we discuss this in the following section.

We suggest that these guidelines be developed jointly by a small group of practitioners, drawn from DoE and the local authorities in consultation with the voluntary sector. The guidelines recently issued for economic development projects might serve as a model.'

The use of such guidelines may help to clarify future thinking, but it will not help with the numerous established projects of the kind described in this report and their future must be a matter of grave anxiety.

The demand for 'innovation'
As has already been noted, the emphasis of the Urban Programme has always been on funding innovatory projects—the implication being that standard activity, whether statutory or voluntary, was more suitable for mainstream funding. This was underlined again in the latest ministerial guidelines on grant aid: '. . . the voluntary sector shall continue to be encouraged and supported, especially in projects which are innovatory, meet social need in a cost-effective way and contribute to the regeneration of the inner area'.[7] However, no one has defined what 'innovative' means. Is it innovative to establish a service in a new area or for a new client group which has already been shown to work well elsewhere? The DoE study asks this question in relation to the appointment of 'area caretakers'

attached to residents' associations in Birmingham. There are seventeen such appointments in Birmingham and the study says:

'...while each will be attached to a separate residents' association, nevertheless, they do the same basic job and cannot be said to be innovative in total. We have the impression that much of the Urban Programme now consists of existing ideas and good practice that is being repeated in new locations. Up to a point this is justifiable—for example, there is increasing pressure to develop additional cultural and community centres for particular ethnic minority groups—but a balance has to be struck. Overall, it would seem highly important for the Programme to retain its capacity to back pioneering and challenging projects.'[8]

This issue was brought out clearly over seven years ago in the Edwards and Batley study[9] and it is still more relevant today. The then Director of the Voluntary Services Unit in the Home Office told the authors that:

'...while two years previously, voluntary agencies could concentrate on innovatory and experimental projects and the sort of work that local authorities could not or would not do, the change in economic circumstances over the past few years—circumstances that have affected the voluntary sector as much, if not more, than others—meant that innovation had become a luxury few could afford. There was no longer any guarantee that money would be forthcoming to continue and consolidate innovative efforts, and the result might therefore be a great waste of money and effort. The need now, as far as the voluntary sector was concerned, was not innovation but more funds simply to continue with their basic tasks. It had, the Director felt, been easier for the voluntary organisations to get grant-aid for innovatory and unusual work than for the day-to-day running of their operations and this, in the present circumstances, was misconceived because there was a growing danger that some agencies simply would not be able to maintain their operations at all, let alone continue with experimental work.'

This is surely an aspect of the Urban Programme which deserves much more attention than it has received. However, if the Programme's innovatory emphasis is maintained, attention needs to be given to means of providing the expertise and the resources to monitor and write up projects in a way which makes them genuinely experimental, so that others can learn from them.

138

Multiple funding

As this report has made clear, the Urban Programme is by no means the only source of funding available. The wide range of potential sources is well described in *Fund-raising: a handbook for minority groups,* published by the Commission for Racial Equality in 1979. Another, more up-to-date source of information is *Government grants: a guide for voluntary organisations,* published by NCVO in 1983. The main point to make here is to re-emphasise the problems, apparent again and again in the course of visiting the projects described in this study, which arise from being forced to use a package of grants with different expiry dates, different criteria for record and account keeping, and different objectives in the grant-giver's mind. The complex and inter-active nature of the process is well described by Mary Tuck in a Home Office Research Bulletin.[10]

'Some (funded organisations) draw funds from as many as thirty different sources within a year. When it is remembered that many funding sources are drawn from the same government purse and many independent sources benefit from government grants and fiscal policies, the immense proliferation and dupli-cation of effort represented by the multiple funding becomes salient. Characteristically, an ethnic minority voluntary organisa-tion will be set up on some very small administrative grant from one source providing some minimal salary or help for a part-time organiser or secretary. This funded person will then spend most of his or her time arranging funding from yet another source, local, national or non-governmental. When several funding sources have been stitched together, the group will be a well-established one, probably running several different activities. The different funding bodies will all wish for reports and accounts, some by the calendar year, some by the financial year. The administrator of the voluntary body finds almost all his time is taken up by meeting the demands of funders. The funding bodies, in turn, find themselves overburdened with paper work, often inefficiently completed, and few of them manage to get out into the field to see what is actually being done with their money. The system is clearly wasteful and inefficient to all concerned.

In defence of it can be argued its freedom from central control. A group refused funding by Urban Aid can apply to the Commis-sion for Racial Equality. One refused by both might be lucky with a private foundation. No one set of administrators is sifting the net in accord with some pre-arranged plan. It is sometimes feared by the more radical members of ethnic minority communities that funding is used as a conscious method of social control. The plurality of sources of funds makes this unlikely. The system is too decentralised to be consciously managed to any specific end. To that extent, it is open to innovation and responsive to demand.'

Most organisations would, however, be prepared to trade this freedom for greater security and less time-wasting.

Use of MSC employees

The vulnerability of projects which combine Manpower Services Commission (MSC) support with urban aid are particularly serious. As we have seen (p. 88) the MSC can decide to withdraw its grant at a week's notice if they consider there has been maladministration, and continuance from year to year can never be guaranteed. Indeed, serious cutbacks took place in the autumn of 1984 when 28 000 training places run by voluntary and community groups under the government's Youth Training Programme (YTP) were axed in order to give school-leavers more chance to work with private enterprise and industry. This represents a 30 per cent cut—from 88 000 to 60 000 places. Even without these arbitrary cuts, MSC funding is very unsatisfactory as a means of providing staff in the voluntary sector, especially for work with older people. The worker has no sooner made friends with the service users and acquired some skills and knowledge than his or her year is up and the organisation has to start again. MSC funding can be effectively used, however, as the West Indian Women's Association in Brent and the United Caribbean Association in Leeds have shown (nos 17 and 29). The SAUS booklet[11] sums up the problems clearly:

'Difficulties ... emerge with all joint funding—Urban Programme, charitable trusts, the Commission for Racial Equality, for example—but our interviews reinforced the widely held view that the most difficult relationship is between Urban Programme and Manpower Services Commission (MSC) support. As others have pointed out, the MSC has a very particular view about its role in supporting a programme of schemes which are concerned with participants in, or entrants into, the labour market. As the experience of several schemes has shown, the aims and criteria of the MSC may well conflict with those of a self-help oriented voluntary organisation which has the individual or the community as its main focus. It is clear also that the style of administration adopted by some MSC officials is often unhelpful for voluntary organisations, with a strong emphasis on procedures, the rule book, and the formal mechanisms of supervision and control. There are, of course, variations between areas (as there are variations between local authorities and between voluntary organisations) and MSC have acted to establish a number of development workers or 'enablers' to assist the emergence of black projects. There remains, however, an impression that collaboration between the Urban Programme and MSC-supported programmes is, at best, uneasy and, at worst, highly unproductive, and we recommend that further attention be devoted by DoE and DE to improving the relationship between MSC programmes and the Urban Programme.'

The GLC and metropolitan counties

Another serious problem in relation to funding is the projected abolition of the metropolitan authorities and the GLC, which have done so much to supplement the Urban Programme and enable essential expansion to take place. The GLC has a particularly good track record in this connection. It has, for example, contributed essential support to the Cypriot Centre in Haringey, the Pepper Pot Club in Notting Hill, the WIWA Club in Brent, the West Indian Senior Citizens Club in Lambeth, the Asian Community Action Group also in Lambeth and the London-Wide Conference of Ethnic Minority Senior Citizens—to take a few examples from this study at random. Hammersmith and Fulham Council, in its response to the government's discussion document, *Streamlining the cities,* makes the point that the GLC has given over £1·25m to voluntary organisations and community groups within the borough, and that the loss of the GLC's ability to direct its Section 137 allocation (the 2p rate which it can allocate at will) to areas of greatest need is a major cause for concern. If the GLC abolition does go through, it will be absolutely essential to make sure that the voluntary sector continues to receive the support which it has provided.

Section 11 funding

Under Section 11 of the Local Government Act 1966 the government offered to pay 75 per cent of the salaries of local authority staff who were employed to meet the special needs of Commonwealth immigrants in areas where they were highly concentrated. In its original form this money was only available to provide services for people who had been in the country for less than ten years. Take-up of the offer has been extremely patchy. Some authorities have made very extensive use of the money, but have often not ensured that staff paid from it were clearly identified and were in fact providing a specialist service; it therefore simply became a means of subsidising wage bills. Other authorities have made comparatively little use of the facility. Overall, however, it has been an important source of extra money for inner city areas and over £90 m was paid out in 1982/83.[12]

In 1983, the Home Office changed the rules so that provision now covers all first-generation Commonwealth immigrants, no matter how long their period of residence may have been, and their children through their school years. However, grants will now only be made available for new posts if the relevance of the post to the needs of immigrants and their children is clearly spelled out and the individual post-holder is readily identifiable and has appropriate skills. Local authorities are encouraged to consult the communities concerned before submitting applications and the posts must form part of a stated strategy for meeting the special needs of Commonwealth immigrants. All existing posts are being reviewed and new posts will be reviewed three years after appointment.

These changes in the rules, and especially the abolition of the ten year rule are of great importance in relation to the provision of services for the elderly, since they make it possible for local authorities to use Section 11 funds to provide staff to meet the needs of elderly settlers from the New Commonwealth who, in many cases, have been in this country for much longer than ten years. Such staff can be used to provide a service run by the local authority for older members of a particular ethnic minority group such as the Calabash Club in Lewisham or Brent's specialist meal services. They can also be used to provide or supplement staff in a service run by a non-statutory organisation on behalf of the council, as Leeds has done (see p. 89); and they can of course be used to pay liaison officers and specialist social workers whose work with a whole community will also benefit elderly people. There are, however problems and disagreements over using Section 11. Some authorities—Birmingham is an example—will not appoint Section 11 workers who have already been approved by the Home Office because the council is operating a policy of rigorous restraint on staff increases. Others, like Wolverhampton, are reluctant to make application because they do not think they can afford their 25 per cent share of the salaries or because they are afraid that Home Office funding may be withdrawn after three years and they will be left with the full bill. Some social services committees, like Leicestershire's, take the view that when additional services or adaptations to existing services are required to meet the needs of elderly people from ethnic minorities, these should be provided 'where possible' within the base budget and not be dependent on the availability of extra funding.[13] This is a point of view that many members of the communities concerned would endorse. But, in spite of its principles, Leicestershire has in fact applied for Section 11 money to fund a number of specialist social work and social work assistant posts for work with elderly people. Appointments may also not be effective in practice because of insufficient preparation and support. A detailed report by an Asian Liaison Officer in Leeds[14] shows that posts may not be properly fitted into the existing staff structure; post-holders may not get the backing they need from senior staff; and their jobs may not be sufficiently defined in terms of role, responsibility and status. If this sort of thing happens, Section 11 appointments can become a token gesture which does more harm than good.

Nevertheless, in spite of its potential for misuse, Section 11 is an important new source of funding for work with elderly Commonwealth settlers and it is important that the ethnic minority communities concerned press local authorities to make full use of it. It is equally important that the local authorities show themselves willing and able to do so.

Conclusion

It has only been possible in this short chapter to draw attention to some of the main issues in an immensely complex, confused and controversial field. Calling attention to the problem is relatively easy, however, compared with the difficulty of actually setting up better procedures for funding and continuing support for ethnic minority services. Any real improvement will demand a great deal of time, good will, determination and money, and, in the end, it will depend on a political decision at central government level. As we have seen, ministerial statements have repeatedly paid lip service to the desirability of encouraging self-help initiatives in the minority communities. If the government now stands back and allows proven time-expired initiatives to collapse for lack of continued funding, and new ones to be still-born because of a block on revenue funding, the hollowness of these statements will be manifest.

The use of government money, whether through urban aid, MSC funds or Section 11 posts must not be allowed to blur the fact that it is the responsibility of local authorities to see that elderly people from ethnic minority groups have access to the services of the

143

same quality and provided at the same level as those provided for the indigenous population. It is evident from the rapid proliferation of voluntary service in this field that investment through community-based initiatives is a quick and effective route to service provision in a situation in which local authorities are not yet able to offer appropriate mainstream services. It is, however, important that if the voluntary sector is used in this way, local authorities should realise that it implies a commitment on their part not only to see that adequate funding is made available but also that the voluntary sector is included in planning and policy formulation. It is also important that local authorities should recognise that use of the voluntary sector to provide basic services is not cheap in terms of staff time. A great deal of work at a senior level may be needed to enable an enterprise to get off the ground and continue to provide a satisfactory service. Use of the voluntary sector is justified for its own sake, but not as a means of providing a cheap service which enables local authorities to evade their basic responsibility to see that all elderly people within their jurisdiction have their needs appropriately met.

SUMMARY OF ACTION REQUIRED

Action by ethnic minority groups
1. Research the case for providing, and therefore for funding, specialist services at the same level as those which are available to the indigenous population and present the facts and figures to councillors.
2. Press the local authority to discuss and clarify its strategy and priorities in putting forward new projects for funding through urban aid, applying for renewal of urban aid grants and using Section 11 finance.
3. Campaign for renewal of grants to provide specialist services well ahead of the expiry of the grant and give attention to publicity and public relations throughout the project.

Action by local authorities
1. Work out a clear policy on the level of base line services which should be provided to *all* elderly people who need them, so that equivalent responsibility to elderly members of ethnic groups can be determined.
2. Define and state the authority's policy on processing urban aid applications, including its attitude to the voluntary sector in general, the 'ethnic dimension' in its strategy, and means of discussing policies and priorities with ethnic minority groups.

3. Simplify and publicise procedures for applying for urban aid and make the process of assessment and decision-making well-known, open and equitable.
4. Review the process of liaison with and evaluation of *all* voluntary organisations using public funds.
5. If renewal of urban aid funding cannot be obtained for basic specialist services, give full consideration to the case for providing an equitable share of mainstream funding even if this means cutting back on other provision.
6. Explore the use of Section 11 money to provide services for elderly people in ethnic minorities.

Action by central government
1. The Department of the Environment should require programme applications to be based on a clearly-stated strategy which recognises ethnic minority group needs.
2. Innovation and encouragement of new initiatives through the Urban Programme should be balanced against the need to create well-tested forms of service and ensure that good projects do not risk loss of continued funding.
3. Projects which are taken onto the mainstream funding from the Urban Programme should be exempted from rate-capping.
4. The current emphasis on capital-intensive and commercial use of urban aid should be reconsidered in relation to specialist voluntary services for ethnic minority groups.
5. The Manpower Services Commission should review its policies in relation to voluntary organisations so that they promote the best interests of both organisations and employees, the possibility of planning services over a reasonably lengthy period, and sensitive, flexible administration.
6. Organisations funded by the GLC and metropolitan counties should be guaranteed full and fair consideration for continued funding.
7. The Home Office should encourage imaginative and flexible use of staff funded through Section 11 to promote the well-being of elderly members of ethnic minorities, including the secondment of staff to work with voluntary organisations.

REFERENCES
1. Murray Stewart and Gill Whitting, *Ethnic minorities and the Urban Programme,* occasional paper no 9, School for Advanced Urban Studies, University of Bristol, 1983.
2. Stuart Elliott, Graham Lomas, Alan Riddell, *Community projects review: a review of voluntary projects receiving Urban Programme funding,* Department of the Environment, London, 1984.

3. Information from Department of the Environment, August 1984.
4. See ref 2.
5. Letter from Hammersmith and Fulham Council, 1984.
6. See ref 2.
7. Department of the Environment. *Inner cities directorate,* DoE, London, 1982.
8. See ref 2.
9. John Edwards and Richard Batley, *The politics of positive discrimination: an evaluation of the Urban Programme 1967–77,* Tavistock Publications, London, 1978.
10. Mary Tuck, 'On researching self-help groups: a problem in evaluation research', *Home Office Research Bulletin* no 8, 1979, p.22.
11. See ref. 1.
12. *Section 11 of the Local Government Act, review of post,* Home Office Circular no 94, 30 August 1983.
13. Leicestershire County Council Social Services Department, *Services for the elderly: a strategy paper,* Leicester 1983.
14. Leeds Community Relations Council, *Section 11 report,* unpublished, Leeds 1984.

CONCLUSION

Members of ethnic minority groups complain, with justification, that they are constantly being subjected to 'research' by sociologists who are motivated by curiosity, fashion, or the availability of funding, rather than by a real concern to lay a foundation for action. This complaint has been particularly voiced by elderly people from the Afro-Caribbean and Asian communities who say that quite enough is known about what improvements in services they want. What is needed now is not more information but more action. This report has sought to take the translation of research into action at least one stage further by attempting to indicate, at the end of every chapter, what needs to be done and who should be responsible for doing it. By itself, however, that will achieve nothing. Elderly people in general are only too accustomed to being on the receiving end of a flow of 'double messages' which acknowledge their rights in theory but deny them in practice. For example, they are constantly being told that they have *earned* the right to respect, decent living conditions and proper care, but another message is often delivered at the same time: 'resources are scarce and the young must have the lion's share—after all, they have their lives before them'. Health service professionals publicly agree that elderly people have a right to have their illnesses properly investigated and treated, but if you go to your GP with a pain or join the queue for surgery, the real message often is 'Well, what do you expect at your age? Don't take up my time or threaten to block one of my precious beds'. In theory, it is agreed that elderly people should be encouraged to participate in learning experiences and share their skills and knowledge with others; in practice, the response they get is likely to be 'if you are old, you must be dotty!'. Elderly settlers are likely to experience all these double messages, together with some others which arise from inevitable gaps between traditional customs and the way the younger generation have to live in Britain. But there is one contradiction between theory and practice which is peculiar to this group. The theory is 'you are equal members of our society with a right to equal consideration and equal use of services'. The practice is 'if you can't make use of what is available, it is just too bad. You will have to go without'.

If we cannot or will not meet particular needs, then we ought at least to have the honesty to say so. But that is a counsel of despair. What must be done is to define and acknowledge the gap between theory and practice and take visible, practicable steps to close it. An ounce of action is worth a ton of sentiment. As the introduction to this report emphasised and the succeeding chapters have demonstrated, there is no simple answer and no single answer. It is up to us all to look for solutions, whether we work in central or local government, the health service, or voluntary organisations, and whether or not we class ourselves as members of a minority ethnic group. But everyone's responsibility all too often becomes no one's responsibility. We simply must not allow this to happen. The statistics quoted in the second chapter of this report and the information coming from the communities themselves constitute an urgent and serious challenge. The necessary preparations to meet that challenge must be made *now*. Elderly people are already experiencing the consequences of the refusal of service providers to face the implications of demographic statistics which could and should have told them twenty years ago that we had got to prepare for unprecedented numbers of very elderly people in our society. If we again refuse to face facts and do nothing to provide services which are accessible to the rapidly growing numbers of elderly settlers, we will be deliberately allowing many of them to grow old in fear and isolation and to die of untreated illness, malnutrition and lack of care.

SUMMARY OF MAIN CONCLUSIONS

1. Many elderly settlers are, through no fault of their own, unable to use many basic services relating to medical treatment, day care, domiciliary support, information provision, libraries etc, as they are provided at present.

2. Health authorities, local authorities and voluntary organisations urgently need to change the way in which they recruit staff, publicise facilities, use interpreters and consult with the ethnic minority communities in their area, so as to make their general service provision more sensitive and more open in the way in which it is offered.

3. Some local authority services, particularly day care, domiciliary care, meals-on-wheels and libraries require specialist provision which is tailored to the particular religious, social, dietary or language requirements of the various ethnic minority groups.

4. The communities concerned can do a great deal to help their own elderly members, both by setting up appropriate specialist facilities in cooperation with the local authorities and by articulating the difficulties which their members encounter in making use of non-specialist services.

5. A specialist voluntary service requires adequate and reliable long-term funding. If the local authority is satisfied that it provides an appropriate and necessary facility which is equivalent to that made available to the indigenous elderly population, then the authority has a moral obligation to see that such funding is made available, if necessary, from the main budget.

6. The Department of the Environment and the local authorities should make every effort to see that urban aid becomes accessible to voluntary organisations within the ethnic minority groups and to encourage a consistent, fully discussed and properly planned use of urban aid in this field, without undue emphasis on 'innovation'.

7. The Department of Health and Social Security should give health authorities and local authorities clear guidance on action required both to 'sensitise' general service provision, and to provide special facilities where these are necessary.

8. Local authority housing departments should urgently review their policy in relation to the provision of specialist sheltered or appropriate housing for elderly members of ethnic minority groups, as should existing housing associations; and the Housing Corporation should give sympathetic consideration to

applications from ethnic minority groups to set up independent housing associations.

9. The government should take urgent steps to rescind the obligation on sponsors of immigrant dependants to maintain and house them without recourse to public funds.

10. All of us must cease to connive at the 'double message' which offers elderly members of ethnic minorities equal use of services in principle, but denies it to them in practice.

Appendix 1
Day centres and clubs visited during the project

Asian day centres and clubs
1. *Scope*
Western Road, Southall, Middlesex   *Tel. 01 574 0902*

Scope Southall is the name of a local Youth Community work project which was established in the Asian community in 1974 to cater
for the needs of the elderly, young people and women. It set up the
Elderly Asian Day Centre in 1980 and after two years of accommodation in a run-down old petrol station, a housing association
provided the project with a large and pleasant detached Edwardian
house. The lease of this has now been purchased with the aid of an
anonymous donation of £85,000. The building is well-decorated
and maintained and has a homely, pleasant atmosphere.

Scope is unique in that it is open seven days a week and for as long
as it is needed each day—from about 10 am to late evening. Its
organisers feel strongly that evenings and weekends are times when
younger people are at home and family life gets most crowded, so it
is then that a refuge is most needed. Attendance averages about 100
a day and 70–80 at weekends. People of any age are accepted, and
with high unemployment they are getting many younger men. There
is no formal membership. 'We would run out of cards if we tried'—
and people come and go as they please. An advisory service is on
constant tap with the main queries about housing, immigration
problems and DHSS benefits. They do not provide meals at present,
though they would like to do so.

The first floor is reserved for the use of women, so they get equal
treatment in terms of accommodation. The emphasis here is much
more activity-centred than for the men, with classes in language,
dressmaking, health education, cooking, crafts and so on, though
both attendance and available teachers have fallen off badly since
MSC funding ceased (see below). There is no particular emphasis
on older women, but an age mix is important in learning and
communicating skills and relieving isolation of both old and young.

Since 1983 this very large undertaking has been running entirely on
voluntary labour, apart from one worker whose salary is paid to
him as warden of a sheltered housing development (see p 48). The
six people engaged in running the club and advice centre (including
those required for cleaning and care-taking) and the eight involved
in the Women's Centre were all MSC employees, and MSC funding
was cut off with less than a week's notice following a dispute
between the MSC and Scope's parent body, the National Association for Asian Youth. Scope itself was not involved in this dispute

and they felt victimised by the local MSC authorities, but neverthe-less they lost all their MSC funding in August 1983 and it has never been reinstated.

2 *Milap Day Centre*   *Tel. 01 574 2311 (ext 223)*
Town Hall Annexe, Southall, Middlesex   *01 843 1893*

The Milap Day Centre operates in council-owned premises—a lightly-built one-storey annexe attached to a disused town hall in Southall High Street. The original initiative came from local auth-ority community workers following three reports on Asian affairs in Southall which highlighted the plight of older people in terms of low income, acute loneliness and alienation. After very lengthy negotiations, the council agreed to make the town hall annexe available, and the centre opened in November 1980 with all the usual activities. A lunch club is now planned. One room is reserved for weekly use by women (there are 40 on the books) for video, language teaching and social interaction, and they come to the festival celebrations, but there is no formal outreach work to women at present.

There are about 600 registered members and an average daily attendance of, about 120 (Monday-Friday) with a strict lower age limit of 60 except for chronically-disabled people who may be admitted at 55. The present warden (a Sikh) was formerly a teacher, but also did a lot of voluntary work. At the time of the visit he had a full-time deputy and four part-time MSC-funded helpers, but hoped to get two more full-time staff using GLC funding, so that the centre can open on Saturdays and deal adequately with the numbers now attending. One of these new employees will be a woman.

3 *The Pensioners' Group, The Asian Centre*
8 Caxton Road, London N22   *Tel. 01 889 6938*

A small self-run club for elderly men meets in this centre which is used by a wide range of Asian organisations. It is a modern building which was originally occupied by the planning team when the Wood Green shopping complex was being built and the main floor is mostly a large open-plan area which can be divided into smaller sections by the use of partitions. There are problems of noise when they are in use simultaneously by different groups. The pensioners' group has the daily use of one partitioned 'room' and, in effect, operates as a card players' club. Though grateful for the hospitality offered, they would very much like to have their own place where they could drop in and which would offer somewhere comfortable to sit with facilities for making refreshments. The club formerly met in a large and bleak church hall and the women's section still meet there because their activity is religious (see below).

4   *Asian Women's Group,*
St Peter's Church Hall, Frobisher Road, London N7

This group is unique in this study, in that it is run by and for older Asian women. The sixty-odd members are all Gujaratis from East Africa and they meet weekly in a huge draughty church hall for religious devotions. A portable shrine which closes up like a triptych is unlocked and opened out for the occasion and a rug spread so that the corner of the hall becomes a little temple. As was noted above, they cannot use the Asian Centre because religious activity is not allowed there. They would dearly love to have a place of their own where the shrine and other furnishing and books could be kept safely and where facilities for refreshments and social activity could be available. Though self-running, the group is supported and encouraged by an Asian community volunteer worker of many years standing. She would like to encourage the group to expand its activities to include the practice of traditional crafts and more social activity, but this has not yet proved possible.

5   *Brent Asian Elders Group, Asian Development Centre,*
186 Church Road, London NW10   *Tel. 01 451 5690/99*

When it was visited, Brent Asian Elders was about to make the transition from shared use of a very run-down community centre to its own much more adequate premises. It runs a day centre with the usual activities, a library with over 1,300 books and a variety of newspapers, an advice service which is available to the community in general, some English language teaching, religious singing and reading, the celebration of festivals and very popular coach trips. Negotiations are also going on with various housing associations to develóp sheltered housing on the ASRA model (see p 46). The new building will have a large upstairs room set aside for women and it is hoped to extend the services available to them after the move.

Lunch is provided from the centralised kitchens of the Council's meals-on-wheels service (see p 106). The availability of this service has in turn been of great importance in encouraging the proliferation of small local Asian clubs in Brent, such as the one described below. It has also proved that acceptable food can be produced by council kitchens if enough trouble is taken.

The group is managed by a committee elected by its members and now has a realistic level of staff, with a full-time community worker and administrator, a part-time co-ordinator and four part-time MSC employees acting as clerical assistant, care assistant, cleaner and driver. It has also obtained a minibus through the Opportunities for Volunteering programme and runs this in association with Brent Community Transport.

6 *Stonebridge Asian Elders Social Group*
The Community Centre, 12 Donovan Court,
Exton Crescent, London NW10   *Tel 01 961 3337*

Stonebridge is a huge, badly designed, high-rise housing estate which epitomises the problems of the inner city. There is a considerable population of older Asians, mainly from East Africa, living in flats which were allocated to them as refugees and which they had no choice but to accept, but whose families have now moved out to buy their own houses.

One of the few assets of the estate is a community centre originally intended as a hostel for mentally handicapped people. This proved impractical because of maltreatment by residents on the estate and the building was taken over by a group of community development workers, who set out to use it as a base for self-help initiatives within each ethnic group. Two small groups of older Asian men meet separately in a cramped room originally intended as a hostel bedroom.

The group visited claims a membership of 50, though the hard core of attenders is very much smaller. It has detailed rules of organis-ation with a president and secretary and its members meet mainly to play cards, chat and eat the vegetarian Asian lunch provided by the council kitchens. Wives are only included at festivals and for religious activity. The group would like to have its own premises and a part-time organiser who could look after administration, negotiate with the council, and help them to develop a mutual sup-port role in visiting the housebound, providing welfare advice and organising outings and social activity. (These ambitions are shared with over twenty similar groups within the borough.)

7   *The Pakistan Centre, Station Parade,*
Willesden Green, London NW2   *Tel. 01 452 4103*

This purpose-built centre, which serves a community of Pakistani
Moslems with a very rural origin, offers youth work, teaching, social events and religious services. Women use the premises on
Saturday and Sunday morning and one weekday afternoon. The
only formal provision for elderly people is a lunch club which provides a meal cooked by a volunteer on one day a week. This is felt to
serve a useful purpose in encouraging older people to drop into the
centre for a cup of tea, a chat and informal advice-giving at other
times. The single-handed organiser feels a deep concern for the
elderly, many of whom, he says, are in a very vulnerable position,
and he would like to be able to extend the facilities and services
offered to them but cannot do this without more help and accommodation. Although purpose-built, the present building has many
faults. The one very large hall looks bleak, as if it was designed as a
gymnasium, with a very high ceiling and exposed roof trusses and
breeze-block walls. There is no space except the entrance foyer for
informal relaxation or games by members of any age group and no
storage space. Intended offices have not yet been built.

The capital cost was funded partly by Urban Aid and partly by the
Pakistani Workers' Association. It is not yet fully paid for, however, and raising further money from the Pakistani community
has proved difficult because, under Urban Aid rules, the freehold
belongs to the council and people are reluctant to put money into
premises in which they only have a leasehold interest.

8   *All-Moslem Women and Children Association*
c/o 57 West Ella Road, Harlesden, London NW10

This association is the creation of a socially-concerned Pakistani
Moslem woman who runs a school teaching traditional knowledge
and skills, for about 40 children in her own home each evening,
and also provides English classes for older women and has a recreational group for mothers with young children and for older
women. In addition, she organises help for mothers who are ill and
runs cultural festivals in hired premises. Through these activities,
she comes to know and provides support to very traditional elderly
Moslem women who are desperately isolated and depressed, and
often on bad terms with their families, but are afraid to live apart
from them.

The organiser has tried to obtain help with the running costs of her activities and with obtaining premises since the use of her home is becoming increasingly unsatisfactory and her work with older children and older women could be greatly expanded if she had more space. Hiring halls for cultural activities is also time-consuming and costly and her telephone bill is enormous. She has, however, experienced much difficulty in obtaining grant aid because her activities cut across the various relevant committees—mixing education, welfare and cultural development—and so do not fit tidily under one administrative label.

9 *Scope Leicester, Belgrave Neighbourhood Centre,*
Rothley Street, Leicester   *Tel. 0533 681638*

Scope originated in 1980 when workers at the Belgrave Neighbourhood Centre became concerned about the plight of elderly Asians living in the area. Eventually, urban aid was granted to create more space within the neighbourhood centre, so that a large room could be set aside for exclusive use by day and a vegetarian lunch is cooked on the premises by two part-time workers and a volunteer. Membership is open to men and women over 50, but activities for women are at present limited to swimming, keep fit, language classes and specific social and religious events.

Particularly noteworthy is the success of Scope's coach trips to places of beauty or interest all over the country, and also holidays in Europe. The six European holidays arranged in 1983 carried fifty people each and were charged at £5 a head more than the actual cost in order to subsidise the outings in Britain, and so make it possible for everyone to take part. These trips are extremely popular with all age groups and indicate what a strong demand there is within the Asian community to widen their horizons and explore their new country, as well as to travel still farther afield.

The management committee, elected by members, employs one full-time worker but the person effectively in charge is the Vice Chairman, Mr G J Ganatra who works more than full-time on the project as a volunteer. Mr Ganatra is a refugee from Uganda who has devoted his life in Britain to the Centre and to other voluntary work. He hopes to extend Scope's activities by using the kitchen, which is being modernised, to provide meals-on-wheels for housebound people and to obtain a minibus which will enable housebound and blind people to be brought into the centre.

156

10   *Clubs run under the auspices of Age Concern Leicester,*
46 Humberstone Gate, Leicester LE1 3PG
St Barnabas Library   *Tel. 0533 24104/5/6*
St Saviour's Neighbourhood Centre
Highfields Community Centre
Moat Community College

These clubs are unusual in that they have been set up by a traditional and white-dominated organisation providing services to the
elderly in general. Age Concern Leicester shows that it can be done,
though it is having difficulty in obtaining further funding for the
project, partly because the social services department are uncertain
as to whether it is right to give money to provide a service for Asians
to an organisation which at the time of writing has no-one from an
ethnic minority on its management committee.

Mr Ben Gamadia, an Asian Christian, was appointed in 1982 with
the help of a CRE grant to investigate needs in two areas of high
Asian concentration in the city. He undertook some exploratory
home visits and a survey, and decided it was necessary to set up separate facilities to meet differing needs. Thus, the club at St Barnabas
Library meets fortnightly with the main objectives of encouraging
use of the library service, improving knowledge of statutory and
voluntary services, showing films and slides and encouraging questions and discussion. One group meeting at the drab 19th-century St
Saviour's Community Centre has the same kind of programme with
a monthly visit from a mobile library designed for use by elderly and
handicapped people and also Asian meals provided by the social
services department. Another group of frail and disabled housebound people are brought in by minibus and also taken on outings
in the town. In spite of the bare surroundings and hard chairs, this
club (which was the only one of the four visited) is evidently much
appreciated and attracts not only attenders but considerable volunteer help from Asian students. The group which meets at the Community College focuses on craft instruction and learning English.
The teacher is herself an elderly East African Asian with 25 years
teaching experience and is particularly successful in encouraging
both Hindu and Moslem women to join the class. Other activities
include a handicraft workshop and yoga classes at the Highfield
Community Centre, a fund-raising theatre event in which young
and old joined to perform a specially-written script, trips to London
and publication of information circulars in Gujarati. A trip to India
is planned.

At the time of the visit, Ben Gamadia was working almost unpaid because the CRE funding had run out, social services were unable to give any financial assistance to the project, and Age Concern Leicester's own budget was stretched to the limit. An application was being made for funding under the Opportunities for Volunteering programme.

11 *Day Centre for the Elderly, The Indian Community Centre, Rawson Street, New Basford, Nottingham*   *Tel. 0602 785985*

The Indian Community Centre is based in a large 19th-century building up a hill and in an industrial area, and so not ideal for access by elderly people. Amongst much other activity, it runs mixed day care for elderly men and women on one day a week. Unlike many of the centres described in this report, it deliberately tries to cater for housebound people. About 50 people, mainly Gujarati, come from all over the city in a ten-seater minibus provided by the social services department. Additional transport is badly needed. A vegetarian lunch is provided by a part-time cook and kitchen assistant funded by Urban Aid.

At the time of the visit, the warden of the Community Centre was running the work for old people himself in addition to all his other duties, but two part-time MSC workers—one man and one woman—were in the process of being appointed and it was hoped that these would take on much of the day-to-day work in providing services for the elderly and do some development work in outreach to people in their own homes. Induction training for these new workers was to be facilitated by the social services department.

12 *The Asian Day Centre, Barrack House,*
45 Barrack Road, Leeds   *Tel. 0532 621035*

This little centre for older Asian men is based in council-owned property also used for children's work in a semi-derelict row of buildings on the bleak edge of the Chapeltown district of Leeds. Externally it could scarcely be less attractive, but the room is homely and well furnished. The project originated in a grant obtained by the Community Relations Council from Urban Aid to fund an experimental Asian meals-on-wheels service. This never got off the ground, but with encouragement by the principal adviser on the elderly in the Leeds social services department, the CRC, with the support of local group community leaders, translated the project into a day centre and lunch club. An Asian woman was appointed to run the centre. She has no particular qualifications, but is a competent, motherly person and does the cooking herself. Her husband, who is retired, provides constant presence and support on a voluntary basis. He owns a car which has proved to be a very useful asset. The atmosphere is friendly and rather paternalistic, with a strong emphasis on 'making older people happy'. The usual activities take place and the centre remains open from 10 am to 6 or 7pm in the evenings on weekdays (the caretaker taking responsibility for locking up). It does have to close on occasion, however, because the room is needed for children's work—for example, during the half-term holiday. The original grant has now run out and the project has gone over to Section 11 funding so the worker has become a council employee.

13 Guru Nanak Sikh Temple, Wakefield Road, Bradford 4

A very large room underneath the temple has been converted with Urban Aid into a hall with a platform for concerts and entertainments. Two long, narrow rooms off each side of this hall are used by elderly men—one as a club room and the other is furnished with beds for emergency use. These rooms cannot be centrally heated, however, without heating the whole building which is prohibitively expensive and the electric fires provided are not adequate. The rooms are also at present minimally furnished and equipped, though a video is available, the grant having been used up on the alterations and on the general high running costs of the building and on buying the video. Premises are supervised by a caretaker who also looks after the temple, but there are no other paid staff. There are facilities for tea-making, but main meals are not normally provided. Probably because of the lack of comfort, the club room is not extensively used at present.

14 Indian Workers Association, 1210 Leeds Road, Bradford 3

The Association owns a small shop-front terraced house with a small clubroom on the ground floor and a kitchenette upstairs. It is used mainly by older Sikh men for chatting and card-playing. No main meal is provided. The club is run entirely on a voluntary basis by the members of the management committee who share responsibility for opening up, closing, cleaning, etc, and hold an advice session.

15   *Birmingham Central Mosque*
180 Belgrave Road, Highgate, Birmingham   *Tel. 021 554 4149*

The Mosque Trust proposes to establish a day centre for elderly Moslems in the basement of the main building. The premises are very extensive and have been specially converted for the purpose using Urban Aid, but at the time of the visit had not been furnished and details of staffing and management had not been worked out. Meals will be cooked on the premises and activities will include religious lectures, prayers, videos or films showing documentaries concerning the Islamic way of life, and recreational games, but no gambling will be allowed. The part of Birmingham in which the mosque is situated has been cleared for development, so there is no immediate local community, and it will be necessary to provide transport and bring people in from a wide area, if the facilities are to be fully used. Married women can accompany their husbands and will have separate provision, but the main emphasis is very strongly on encouraging elderly men in religious understanding and practice.

16   *Elderly Asian Day Centre,*
Clarence House, Clarence Road, Wolverhampton   *Tel 0902 773580*

Wolverhampton Community Relations Council became so concerned about the situation of older Asian men who had nowhere to go during the day that they started this day centre in two small rooms at the back of their own offices. They have however been unable to obtain any revenue funding and in consequence furnishing and decoration are more run-down than in any premises seen in the course of this project. There is also no money for a paid organiser and the CRC staff make out as best they can while doing their normal work. It says much about the desperation of the members that they are prepared to use the centre. The local authority did put up £1,000 to provide a video and TV set, but refused more on the grounds that the premises and provision were so poor that they could not justify putting more money into them—a Catch 22 situation. Thirty or forty people attend daily, but the CRC workers say that there are many more in need of day centre facilities and are at serious risk through alcoholism, chronic illness, danger of mugging, cold and bad housing.

Afro-Caribbean day centres and clubs
17   *West Indian Women's Association,*
lunch club at 71 Pound Lane, London NW10   *Tel. 01 451 4827*

The West Indian Women's Association (WIWA) was set up in 1977 with the aim of keeping Afro-Caribbean culture alive and enabling older people to pass it on to their children and grandchildren. The Association (which now includes men) had a long struggle to get premises, but is now a large and flourishing organisation with eight permanent members of staff, funded from various sources, plus an MSC scheme with two senior workers and 33 trainees. Some of these MSC workers are used by other ethnic minority groups including the Asian Elders Group (see no 5). WIWA's premises are not big enough to accommodate the lunch club which meets in the hall of a former school made over by the Council for use by various groups within the Afro-Caribbean community. The arrangement is not ideal, however, and WIWA would like to have services for all age groups under one roof so that the age gap can be bridged and young and old can help each other and share the use of a sitting room, video films and so on. They would also like to have space for craftwork and sewing and to provide physiotherapy. A physiotherapist does attend once a week, but present facilities make it difficult for her to give individual treatments. There are 57 members on the lunch club's register and about 40–45 attend daily—most have to be collected as the centre's location is inconvenient and they come from all over the Borough. WIWA owns two eleven-seater minibuses which are also used by the youth groups in the evening and transport is provided free. Lunch is cooked on the premises.

18   *The Welcome Senior Citizens Club,*
Neasden Methodist Church Centre, Neasden Lane North,
London NW10

This club caters specifically for disabled people and accepts members of any age though most are middle-aged or elderly. About 150 are on the books and about 35 are brought in four days a week, transported in two minibuses owned by the club—the vehicles are also used to take meals to housebound people. Accommodation is in modern premises attached to a Methodist church but space is very limited; there is no room for activities, handicrafts, or storage, and the kitchen is not equipped for storing food bought in bulk and is too small for large-scale cooking. The club has now obtained a grant to provide its own purpose-built premises. As with many of the Afro-Caribbean initiatives the club owes its existence to the energies of one individual, Mrs B. Maynard. She now acts as welfare officer, undertaking extensive work which goes well beyond members of the club and includes advice giving, liaison with statutory services and outreach to housebound people. There is also a co-ordinator, driver, care attendant, cook and part-time cleaner, all funded through Urban Aid.

19   *New Testament Church of God Pensioners Club,*
Lambert Road, London SW2 2BB   *Tel. 01 737 0963*

This little day centre, which operates without external funding, has been set up in premises created by the simple expedient of roofing in a gap between the main church building and a boundary wall. A door was put in one end, and a vestibule opened up and made into a small kitchen at the other. (The planning authorities were not consulted and when they eventually arrived they did not have the heart to knock it down.) The centre opens for a full day once a week and caters for nearly 30 people of whom about a third are men. There is a strong sense of self-help with members teaching each other their skills and sharing in the preparation of lunch. Members do not have to have any connection with the Church but a no-smoking rule, which is part of the church discipline, is strictly enforced. The general atmosphere is exceptionally friendly and relaxed. The main church which is a huge Victorian building, has had an extra floor put in to provide space for youth work and social events and it is hoped eventually to install a lift and so enable older people to use this new resource. It will be interesting to see whether the friendly, homely atmosphere in the present makeshift quarters survives this move.

20   *Senior Citizens Club, West Indian Senior Citizens Association,*
117 Railton Road, London SE2   *Tel. 01 737 3505*

The West Indian Senior Citizens Association (WISCA) in Brixton is one of the pioneers in club provision for older Afro-Caribbeans and, with 538 members at the time of the visit, is also one of the largest. The club/day centre is staffed by a manager, care assistant, outreach worker, part-time cook, part-time kitchen assistant and part-time cleaner, all funded through Urban Aid. Considerable difficulty is experienced in covering the workload, however, especially during times of staff absence. This is one of the very few centres visited in the course of preparing the report which has its own fully-

162

converted and equipped premises—put together from three terraced
houses with shop-fronts but modernised so that from the front they
look purpose-built. The ground floor, which is accessible to wheel-
chair users, comprises sitting, dining and kitchen space, and the first
floor has rooms for a wide variety of activities including a library/
reading room (run in association with the council library service),
dressmaking, crafts, and quiet conversation. There is also a well-
furnished committee room. The top floor provides offices which are
used by the outreach worker attached to the centre and also by
workers with the Brixton Neighbourhood Community Association
(BNCA). One of these offices is occupied by BNCA's deputy director, Mrs Ruby Laws, who pioneered WISCA's development and is
still closely involved with its work, but also has charge of youth
and community work and the training of students in placement with
the BNCA. This shared use is an interesting development and the
flexibility of the building will become still more evident when, as is
planned, the basement is opened as a licensed club to which older
Afro-Caribbeans can bring their families for a relaxed afternoon or
evening. Although the Centre is accessible to disabled people, suitable transport is not available and this is badly needed. WISCA is
an independent offshoot of BNCA with its own executive committee. Though the centre is the main focus of its activities, its
members also take part in a considerable amount of outreach supportive care of people in their own homes and in hospital through a
visiting scheme organised by a sub-committee of members. Other
sub-committees organise entertainment, fund-raising and outings (in
the centre's own coach) and, of course, the work of the centre itself.
A general meeting of centre members is held once a week. Mrs Laws
also runs a counselling session on one day a week. The modernis-
ation of the centre's buildings was funded with Urban Programme
and Trust money and MSC labour was used to assist in the construction. But the building, with its final triumphant opening by
the Queen Mother, was only achieved after a very long struggle to
convince Lambeth Council of the need and after a run-down community centre previously used for the club had literally collapsed
(fortunately at night).

WISCA is also of interest for the way in which it remains closely
associated with BNCA, but yet keeps its separate identity. Achieving a balance between maintaining a relationship with a wider
ethnic minority 'umbrella' group and in self-determination for an
organisation whose primary concern is with elderly people is an
important aspect of development in this field.

21 Brixton Seventh Day Adventist Church Lunch Club, Santley Street, London SW4

This centre is run in a church hall which has been made as homely as possible through the use of screens, rugs and curtains. The day opens and closes with prayers. Limited temporary funding from Age Concern England pays for heating and a part-time cook, and Help the Aged has provided a minibus but the centre has no subsidy for meals and relies heavily on volunteers for its day-to-day running. It had not been open for long when it was visited and many of the hoped-for activities were not yet off the ground. However, the emphasis is on practical help as well as crafts and entertainment, and it is hoped to have talks on welfare and health matters and a regular session with a health visitor to talk to individuals about their health anxieties.

22 Caribbean Senior Citizens Association, 39 Cranwich Road, London N16 5H2   Tel. 01 802 6111

This group is unusual in that it is a self-help initiative with no single dominant organiser. It is run by an elected volunteer committee, and the chairman, secretary and a committee member gave a joint interview when asked to talk about their plans. The group has been meeting monthly on borrowed premises for four years and has only just obtained the use of working space at a newly-opened community centre on two days a week. They have had no external funding at all except a little which the local Community Relations Council, which has been very supportive, has managed to make available and they feel they too are in a 'catch 22' situation in which they cannot get funding because they are 'not sufficiently active' and cannot be active because they cannot get funding. They emphasise how difficult it is to get things off the ground with no organisational expertise and only volunteer help, and would like to have a paid worker to undertake administrative and development work. Given premises and some administrative back-up, they feel that their members could do a great deal to help each other.

23 The Pepper Pot Club, 140 Ladbroke Grove, London W10   Tel. 01 962 2433

The Pepper Pot Club is unusual in that it developed from a Citizen's Advice Bureau community service. The community worker, Mrs. Pansy Jeffrey, recognised the isolation and loneliness among the older Afro-Caribbean people she encountered during her CAB

164

work and started using the community service office as a drop-in centre which served unemployed people and those in early retirement as well as pensioners. This developed into an activity centre, doing a wide variety of high quality craft work and then into a lunch club. For 19 months the cooking was done by Mrs Jeffrey, her CAB colleagues and volunteers, but there are now three part-time workers employed under the MSC Community Enterprise scheme. The work is now extending to home visiting using specially recruited volunteers (see p 101) and the club will shortly move to its own premises on a new housing estate.

24   Hackney Educational and Development Society (HEADS) Day Centre, 128 Rectory Road, London N17   Tel. 01 249 6061

This started as a monthly club for people who felt socially isolated on retirement, but is now open as a day centre two days a week and is being increasingly used as a drop-in centre on other days. It still retains the informality of its origins since its initiator, Mrs Bledman, is strongly antagonistic to red tape of any kind. There is, therefore, no age limit, no formal membership and no membership fee. Besides the usual craft and other activities there is a strong emphasis on arranging group visits to places of interest in the West End of London and on joining in ILEA classes on activities such as photography, creative writing and running a newspaper. They also go as a group to take part in badminton, swimming, bowls and other sports at the Leisure Centre. This often gives members confidence to undertake such activities on an individual basis.

The club has sole day-time use of a large, dilapidated corner-house owned by HEADS, but the main clubroom is on the first floor. Some members have a painful struggle to get up there, and while doing so, put a dangerous strain on the inadequate bannister. Lavatory facilities are also unsuitable for disabled people. More suitable premises and transport facilities are urgently needed.

Two paid organisers are employed but lunch is bought and cooked by a rota of volunteer club members. With numbers growing all the time, they would like to employ a cook and also a part-time receptionist. This would free the paid staff and Mrs Bledman (who is a virtually a full-time volunteer) for advisory work, taking time to talk to individuals on a personal level, home visiting and hospital visits.

25   The Senior Citizens Friendly Association, 78 Heathfield Road, Handsworth, Birmingham   Tel. 021 551 1942

The Jamaican Community Service Group started planning to establish a day centre for the elderly in 1977, but it did not get off the ground until 1981. After starting off in the hall of a community centre, the project is now based in a corner house on a terraced street which also provides accommodation for various other community groups and is already too small for the 45 people who now attend on an average day. Discussions are now going on with a housing association about the possibility of a combined housing/day centre project. From the start, the emphasis has been on self-help and involving members in decision-making about the club and its activities. A support group, drawn from the membership, work as volunteers in running the project, which also has an elected committee. Only light refreshments are available. It is noteworthy that, as well as varied craft activity for women, a workshop in a shed in the tiny back yard gives male members an opportunity to practise their carpentry skills and especially picture-frame making. Like the centre run by Wesleyan Holiness Church (no 26), the Association is used by the local psychiatric hospital to help in re-socialising Afro-Caribbean psychiatric patients who may have great difficulty in being accepted back into their community. This use of the centre is not age-related and the contact is two-way, in that centre members are invited to go on hospital outings.

26   The Day Centre, Wesleyan Holiness Church, Holyhead Road, Handsworth, Birmingham 21   Tel. 021 523 7849

This huge nineteenth-century church has a large hall and extensive additional accommodation which it uses to provide a day centre for Afro-Caribbean people aged 50 and upwards. The project has been open since May 1983 and runs with funding from the Urban Programme, five MSC staff (cooks, driver and helpers) and various volunteers. A Commission for Racial Equality (CRE) grant paid for some of the extra furniture and equipment required. The centre is open from 8.30–5 pm on five days a week, though most people attend from about 11 am to 3 pm, and it offers an impressive and imaginative range of crafts for both men and women, with an emphasis on encouraging simultaneous occupation and conversation. It is noteworthy that the local psychiatric hospital has successfully used the club for re-socialising both white and black patients. One member of the centre serves on the management committee but as with many church-based facilities the approach is a benevolent paternalism. Disabled people are catered for, but this would be made much easier if a minibus with a tail-lift was available.

27 Cottage of Content Day Care Centre,
Kyrwicks Lane, Sparkbrook, Birmingham   *Tel. 021 771 0764*

The Cottage of Content is a substantial detached house belonging to the city council and used for a wide variety of community activities. The centre, which opened in May 1983 is an offshoot of a Seventh Day Adventist church; its two part-time staff are funded by Urban Aid. It is open on two days a week and provides games, keep-fit and other activities plus a lunch produced by a volunteer cook and paid for by members with no council subsidy. About 17 people come on the most popular day. Most clients are single and living on their own and there are some white attenders. There is considerable outreach in terms of visiting housebound people and providing personal care, shopping, company and general support, and meals are taken to a few housebound people on an informal basis.

28 United Caribbean Association,
12 Hall Lane, Leeds 7   *Tel. 0532 623851*

The association, which is housed in a large detached house on the edge of Chapeltown, started in 1964 as a self-help group mainly concerned with students and housing problems. It has since generated many initiatives which have become independent organisations. Current work is divided between facilities for children, including a Saturday school and holiday care, and work with old people. The latter had only been running for seven months at the time of the visit, but had developed considerably using MSC funding, and now employs two cooks, four care assistants, a caretaker/cleaner, an activity organiser and a manager. The centre is open for five days a week and caters for 32 people a day. Some of these are white and clearly feel that they are getting a degree of concern and care which would not be available to them elsewhere. The emphasis is very strongly on outreach as well as providing care in the centre, and the care assistants spend a lot of time visiting people in hospital and providing personal care in people's own homes. There is more emphasis on physical help to very frail and disabled people than in most of the centres reviewed in this study. A bath on the premises enables people to be given help with bathing and staff will also do personal laundry. A volunteer using his own car, with mileage paid by the social services department, brings people in. It is of interest that the association values its independence too strongly to attempt to get Section 11 funding which would result in staff becoming council employees, and that in spite of the disadvantages of annual changes of staff, they do at present work successfully with MSC funding.

Cypriot clubs
29 *Cypriot Elderly and Handicapped Group, c/o The Cypriot Centre, Earlham Grove, London, N22*   *Tel. 01 341 1100 (am)*
01 881 2329 (pm)

This group began in 1979 and was organised by the Haringey Cypriot Liaison Officers. It met weekly in the Social Services Centre, Willoughby Road. As numbers expanded Cypriot volunteers were brought in to help, and council transport was used once a week to bring in more handicapped members. Soon the meeting room was bursting at the seams and in October 1982 the group was moved to the reception area of the recently opened Cypriot Community Centre in Wood Green—a huge building still only very partially renovated, which was formerly a school. After a few months it became apparent that provision on two days a week was quite inadequate and that the project also needed its own minibus. The Project Team, comprising the liaison officers and present organiser applied for a grant to the GLC and in January 1984 this was granted. This has now enabled the group to function five days a week.

Two full-time workers have been appointed, one organiser and one co-organiser outreach worker who, apart from running the group, arranging outings and providing an advice and casework service, also undertake an increasing amount of work with people in their own homes. A group aide/driver and group aide/escort have also been funded by the GLC and a 15-seater minibus has been purchased with help from the GLC grant and from Age Concern. The group is an independent one which uses the facilities of the Cypriot Community Centre. It is not possible to provide lunches, as the centre itself has not yet got a kitchen or dining-room, so opening hours are 12 noon–4 pm.

The response to these developments has been enthusiastic and in July 1984 membership stood at 335 and included both Greek and Turkish Cypriots. A strong sense of group membership has developed and there is an active executive committee. More activities are available for men than for women at present, but it is hoped that another large room will soon become available where a range of activities acceptable to the women members can be developed. The club is particularly noteworthy for the use made of a grant obtained from the GLC to take members on outings to see places and entertainments which they had never had the opportunity to explore before. These trips have included visits to the Tower of London, Madame Tussaud's, the Commonwealth Institute, London Zoo, the Regent's Park Mosque, Clacton and Brighton, as well as to 'Hello Dolly' and a pantomime.

The evident popularity and very rapid growth of this club is some indication of the tremendous unmet need among older members of the Cypriot community for social contact and recreation, but it has also shown that there are now a considerable number of very elderly Cypriots with an acute need for specialist domiciliary care and sheltered housing.

Jewish Clubs and Day Centres
30   *South West London Friendship Club,*
Lily Montague Hall, Prentis Road, London SW16

31   *South London Jewish Blind Club,*
Cavendish House, Dulwich Road, London SE24

32   *Wembley Care Society,*
c/o Mrs Radbil, 51 Barnway, Wembley, Middx.

33   *North-West London Jewish Day Centre,*
Michael Sobell House, Limes Avenue, London NW11 9JD

These four clubs are discussed together as an illustration of the immense range of voluntary day care made available by the Jewish community to relieve loneliness and provide activity for their own elderly people.

At one end of the scale there is the small 'friendship club' often meeting, as the South West London Friendship Club does, on only one afternoon a week in premises attached to a synagogue and offering light refreshments but not a cooked meal. Usually some kind of entertainment is provided during the afternoon. Some of these clubs have a long history. This one has been going for 31 years with ups and downs of membership, but an average of about 20. There seem to be relatively few male attenders and Michael Jimack, who has done a detailed survey of day care and club facilities in

South London, suggests that this may be because the organisers and volunteers are usually women (see p 44, ref 4). Involving more retired men at this level might help to even the balance. Jimack would also like to see these clubs moving towards providing a mid-day meal. Transport is always a problem, but some people are brought in by volunteers using their own cars.

The South London Jewish Blind Club is very similar in the refreshment and activity offered, but it meets in the lounge of a sheltered housing complex rather than in the hall of a synagogue, is run by a professional social worker employed by the Jewish Blind Society and has a very wide catchment area as membership is only open to people with a visual handicap. Transport is a major problem and voluntary provision has to be supplemented by taxis paid for by the Society. A club of this kind raises interesting issues relating to the best means of meeting the needs of people with particular types of disability who are also members of ethnic communities. For example, should energies be directed towards helping them to make use of non-specialist facilities rather than towards a separate service? If a separate service is necessary, how can the special help which it offers continue to be provided when the number of potential members within a realistic catchment area does not make a special club a viable proposition?

The Wembley Care Society differs from both the above in a number of ways. It is an independent organisation and, like many of the initiatives described in this Appendix, the work of one energetic and caring individual—Mrs F. Radbil. Mrs Radbil pioneered the provision of kosher meals-on-wheels in the Brent area, but soon concluded that people needed to be able to eat together rather than alone in their homes and eight years ago she started a day centre open on two days of the week and based in a large Scout hut. Transport is provided by volunteer drivers, a Brent Council minibus and Brent Community Transport, and although meals are provided from the kosher meals service, all serving and administration is voluntary. The atmosphere is extremely lively and friendly with about 60 people attending on the busier of the two days. Members pay a small amount towards the basic cost of food and rent, and when more money is needed a fund-raising event is laid on. This very individualistic one-off provision has a maternal and authoritarian element which would be off-putting to some people, but it provides a service which is certainly much valued. It is hoped to develop the work of the society further by building sheltered accommodation.

Finally, the centre based at Michael Sobell House illustrates day care provision on a really large scale and provides a model from which all service providers can learn a great deal. This centre, which now has a daily attendance of nearly 250 people, started as a small service in Swiss Cottage run entirely by volunteers. The Jewish Welfare Board and Jewish Blind Society then joined forces to enable it to move to a huge building, formerly a convent school, in Golders Green, but it has never lost the tradition of using volunteers to carry real responsibility and do skilled tasks. There are now 180 volunteers and 20 paid staff and the difference between them is not of role or status, but that the volunteers work shorter hours on a job-sharing basis. Everyone has a proper job description and contract, and volunteers are encouraged to see their work as a privilege rather than 'doing good'. Indeed, many have found their work a lifesaver after bereavement or divorce.

The clientele represents the full range of social class, income and former occupation and membership is open to anyone of pensionable age, to younger people if they are disabled and also to a group of younger psychiatric patients requiring rehabilitation. Opportunities for arts and crafts of many kinds are available, but the management believe that these often get over-emphasised in day centre activity 'as a hangover from occupational therapy'. Activities therefore include the opportunity for more intellectual occupation, including regular discussion groups, debates on controversial issues, bridge playing, concerts, lectures followed by lively question sessions, drama classes, musical appreciation, choral singing, Hebrew and Yiddish teaching, and much more. The atmosphere, as may be imagined, is extremely lively, but there is also a strong element of personal provision and support for those who need it and the centre copes with a considerable number of people in severe confusional states. However, the emphasis is on fitting each individual into the setting in which he or she feels most comfortable, rather than arranging particular services for particular types of people. Services on offer include a large hairdressing salon staffed by volunteer professionals and a dress shop, also with volunteer professional management, which sells good quality clothes, bought straight from the wholesalers. Two other shops sell gifts and kosher foodstuffs, including ready-packed meals. Transport is provided, if necessary, using three minibuses belonging to the centre, volunteers in their own cars and some local authority vehicles, but it is a 'never-ending problem'.

Three other large day centres have been established by the London Jewish Welfare Board in Stamford Hill, Stepney and Redbridge and equally impressive initiatives exist in other parts of the country. Although these undertakings are caring for many people who would otherwise require statutory provision, financial support from the local authorities is minimal and a great deal of money is raised by the Jewish community to keep them going.

Appendix 2

Organisations mentioned in the text, excluding voluntary day centres and clubs

---

1 Age Concern England, Bernard Sunley House, 60 Pitcairn Road, Mitcham, Surrey CR4 3LL *01 640 5431*

2 Age Concern Brent, 120 Craven Park Road, London NW10 *01 965 7711*

3 Age Concern Greater London, 54 Knatchbull Road, London SE5 9QY *01 737 3456*

4 Age Concern Lambeth, 1/5 Acre Lane, London SW2 *01 274 7722*

5 Age Concern Leicester, Clarence House, 46 Humberstone Gate, Leicester LE1 3PJ *0533 24104*

6 All Faiths for One Race (AFFOR), 173 Lozells Road, Lozells, Birmingham B19 1RN *021 523 8076*

7 Arram House, 217 Romford Road, Forest Gate, London E7

8 Asian Community Action Group, Advice/Counselling Centre, 15 Bedford Road, London SW4 *01 733 7494*

9 Asian Resource Centre, 101 Villa Road, Handsworth, Birmingham B19 *021 523 0580*

10 Asian Sheltered Residential Accommodation (ASRA), 5 Westminster Bridge Road, London SE1 7XW *01 928 9379*

11 ASRA Housing Association Ltd, 34 Princess Road West, Leicester LE1 6TJ *0533 544863*

12 Birmingham Voluntary Service Council, Inner City Unit, 161 Corporation Street, Birmingham B4 6PT

13 Brent Irish Advisory Service, 269 Willesden Lane, London NW2

14 The Calabash Centre, George Lane, Lewisham, London SE13

15 Carib Housing Association Ltd, 122 Ashley Gardens, London SW1

16 Centre for Ethnic Minorities Health Studies, Field House Teaching Centre, Duckworth Lane, Bradford BD9 6RJ *0274 490324*

17 Chinese Information and Advice Centre, 152–156 Shaftesbury Avenue, London WC2 *01 836 8291* and *01 379 5098*

18   Citizens Advice Bureau (Chapeltown), New Roscoe Methodist Church, Francis Street, Leeds 7   *0532 629479*

19   Commission for Racial Equality, Elliot House, 10–12 Allington Street, London SW1   *01 828 7022*

20   Community Health Group for Ethnic Minorities and Ethnic Switchboard, 28 Churchfield Road, London W3   *01 993 6119*

21   Family Welfare Association, 501 Kingsland Road, London E8 *01 254 6251*

22   Forum on the Rights of People to Education, c/o Age Concern England (see no. 1)

23   Haringey Community Relations Council, 14a Turnpike Lane, London N8 0PT   *01 889 6871*

24   Help the Aged Housing Trust, 175 Gray's Inn Road, London WC1X 8UX   *01 278 6571/80*

25   Irish Centre, 52 Camden Square, London NW1   *01 485 0051*

26   Jewish Blind Society, 221 Golders Green Road, London NW11 9DW   *01 458 3282*

27   Jewish Welfare Board, 221 Golders Green Road, London NW11 9DW   *01 458 3282*

28   Hackney Pensioners Link, 16 Dalston Lane, London E8 *01 249 8920*

29   Haringey Pensioners Link, Annexe B, Tottenham Town Hall, Approach Road, London N15   *01 808 1000*

30   Harlesden Community Care Project, c/o 13 Nicoll Road, London NW10

31   Institute of Race Relations, 247 Pentonville Road, London N1 *01 837 0041*

32   Leeds Community Relations Council, Centenary House, 59 North Street, Leeds   *0532 430696*

33   Local Authorities Race Relations Information Exchange (LARRIE), 100 Park Village East, London NW1   *01 828 7055*

34   Milan House, c/o Scope, 20 Western Road, Southall, Middx *01 574 0902*

35 Minorities Resource Centre, 2 Alum Rock Road (1st Floor), Saltley, Birmingham B8 1JB *021 326 6696*

36 Multi-Faith Resource Unit, 1 College Walk, Selly Oak, Birmingham *021 472 0139*

37 National Association of Citizens Advice Bureaux, 110 Drury Lane, London WC2 *01 836 9226*

38 National Council for Voluntary Organisations, 26 Bedford Square, London WC1B 3HU *01 636 4066*

39 National Extension College, 18 Brooklands Avenue, Cambridge CB2 2HN *0223 316644*

40 National Federation of Self-Help Organisations, 150 Townmead Road, London SW6 *01 731 4483/9*

41 Nightingale House, Nightingale Lane, London SW12 *01 673 3495*

42 Policy Studies Institute, 100 Park Village East, London NW1 *01 387 2171*

43 Polish Church Committee, 48 Pitts Road, Slough, Berks S4 3XH

44 Training in Health and Race, 18 Victoria Park Square, London E2 9PF *01 980 6263*

45 St James' Hospital, Lockway Road, Portsmouth PO4 8LD *0705 735211*

46 Standing Conference of Ethnic Minority Senior Citizens (London), 5–5a Westminster Bridge Road, London SE1 7XW *01 928 8108 (ext 34)* and *01 928 0095*

The Urban Programme
(This account is an amended version of NCVO Information Sheet
no 27 prepared by Paul Hodson of the NCVO Urban Unit and
reproduced here by permission.)

The Urban Programme is by far the most impressive source of
government money for innovative voluntary and community projects. It is putting £62 million into such projects for the year
1984/85. The actual distribution of Urban Programme money
depends on complex interactions between central government, local
government and the voluntary sector. This information sheet
outlines what the Urban Programme is, how it works, and what
voluntary organisations can use it for.

What is the Urban Programme?
The Urban Programme aims to combat economic, environmental
and social problems through innovative projects. The government
has defined certain areas of the country as suffering from severe
problems and it uses the Urban Programme to direct extra
resources to these areas. The Programme was established by the
Local Government Grants (Social Needs) Act 1969 and expanded
by the Inner Urban Areas Act 1978.

The Department of the Environment (DoE) administers the Programme. In the financial year 1983/84 it is using it to grant £288
million to local authorities. Local authorities may spend this money
on their own projects or grant it to voluntary and community
groups. Either way they must pay 25 per cent of the cost of each

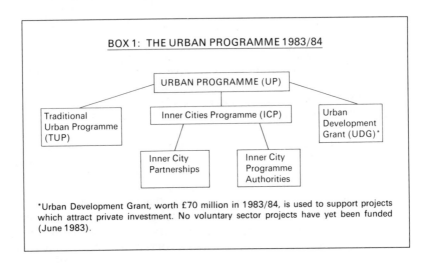

BOX 1: THE URBAN PROGRAMME 1983/84

URBAN PROGRAMME (UP)

Traditional Urban Programme (TUP)

Inner Cities Programme (ICP)

Urban Development Grant (UDG)*

Inner City Partnerships

Inner City Programme Authorities

*Urban Development Grant, worth £70 million in 1983/84, is used to support projects
which attract private investment. No voluntary sector projects have yet been funded
(June 1983).

project from their own funds, with the DoE grant providing the other 75 per cent. And DoE must approve each project.

Where does the Urban Programme operate?

'Urban Programme' is a term which covers several different systems of funding which apply in different areas. The two most important are the Traditional Urban Programme and the Inner Cities Programme (see Box 1).

The Inner Cities Programme covers two sets of local authorities— 'Programme' and 'Partnership' authorities.

The Traditional Urban Programme

The Traditional Urban Programme (TUP) is broad and shallow. It is called 'traditional' because it is the remnant of the original Urban Aid Programme introduced in 1969. In 1983/84 £18 million of new money was allocated for 474 projects. Projects were funded in more than a third of England's 365 shire districts, metropolitan districts and London boroughs. Since then, DoE has reduced the amount and spread of TUP funding, limiting it in most cases to towns with a population of 20,000 or more. Of the projects funded in 1983/84 60 per cent were voluntary.

The Inner Cities Programme

In 1979 TUP was supplemented by funding at a higher level for areas which the government had granted the special status of Programme or Partnership Authorities. (See Box 2). This part of the Urban Programme is known as the Inner Cities Programme.

The key idea behind the Inner Cities Programme is co-ordination. The new Programme aims to give different statutory authorities, and voluntary and commercial bodies too, a financial incentive to come together. They then identify inner city problems, devise policies to solve them and carry these policies out.

For this reason each authority to which ICP is appropriate has to produce an Inner Area Programme (IAP) to accompany its annual list of projects to be funded. IAPs identify needs, policies and priorities. County, district and health authorities are expected to co-ordinate work on the IAP, and 'the community' is supposed to be consulted. In Partnership authorities there is over all a Partnership Committee chaired by a government minister. However, many people now see the Inner Cities Programme simply as a source of

```
BOX 2:  Partnership and Programme authorities

PARTNERSHIPS
Birmingham        Liverpool
Hackney           Manchester and Salford (joint Partnership)
Islington         Newcastle and Gateshead (joint Partnership)
Lambeth

PROGRAMME AUTHORITIES
Blackburn*              Leeds              Sunderland
Bolton                  Leicester          Tower Hamlets*
Bradford                Middlesbrough      South Tyneside
Brent*                  Nottingham         North Tyneside
Coventry*               Oldham             Wandsworth*
Hammersmith and Fulham  Rochdale*          Wirral
Hull                    Sandwell*          Wolverhampton
Knowsley*               Sheffield

*given Programme status in February 1983
```

money and it is certainly still a crucial source for the voluntary
sector.

Unlike TUP, Inner City Programme authorities receive a specific
allocation of money for each financial year. In 1983/84 the seven
Partnerships were each allocated between £12 million and £23 million. The fifteen existing Programme authorities were allocated
between £3 million and £5 million. Eight new areas were given Programme status in February 1983. In 1983/84 these had £1 million to
spend and in 1984/85 they were brought up to the others' level.

What sort of projects get funded?
Inner Cities Programme authorities must divide their allocations
between three categories—economic, environmental and social.
Broadly speaking, when the DoE speaks about economic schemes it
means schemes which aim to encourage job creation—mini-factory
units, for example, or access roads to industrial estates.
'Environmental' schemes include housing and general environmental improvements. Most voluntary projects come in the 'Social'
category, which includes community development, projects for old
or handicapped people, the arts and children's play areas. Although
the present government has shifted the emphasis towards economic
and environmental schemes, projects of all three kinds are still being
supported.

Grants range from under £1000 to over £100,000. In the Traditional Urban Programme there is a maximum of £40,000 for revenue funding and £160,000 for capital funding. In the Inner Cities Programme there is no maximum, though most voluntary schemes are below these limits.

How does the Urban Programme work?

The Urban Programme works differently in each area it covers. What happens depends on the way central government, local government and the voluntary sector interact. But there are certain key things any group needs to know to use the Programme effectively.

Who to apply to

Different local government departments sponsor voluntary sector Urban Programme projects. But the first point of application is most commonly the chief executive's department of the shire district council, metropolitan district council or London borough in which the project will operate. It is also possible to apply at county level, especially for personal social service projects in shire counties, where social services are run by the county. District health authorities can sponsor community health projects in ICP authorities.

When to apply

Both TUP and ICP have an annual cycle. DoE decides which projects it will support for each financial year during the last months of the preceding financial year.

In turn local authorities arrange their own application schedules to fit this cycle. TUP authorities send their bids to DoE in the autumn, and usually ask voluntary organisations to submit bids in the early summer for the following financial year. ICP authorities and some TUP ones publicise their schedule for bidding and for assessing bids.

Who decides what happens?

First, local authorities decide which schemes to submit to DoE. Officers and councillors will be involved, from both the sponsoring department and central bodies (eg the chief executive's department and the policy and resources committee). They may consult voluntary sector representatives (usually via the council for voluntary service (CVS) and community relations council) and it is good practice to invite people to talk about their own project.

Second, DoE decides which schemes to approve. They will take comments from other interested government departments and from regional arms of government, such as regional offices of the DoE and the DHSS. In the Inner Cities Programme there is a third stage. Most authorities have more projects approved than they are allocated money for, and must therefore make a further selection of projects to fund.

It often pays voluntary organisations to lobby for their projects, and to find out who the key people are locally and regionally.

Some ins and outs of Urban Programme funding
Any organisation wanting to get a project funded through the Urban Programme needs to know about revenue/capital balances, 'slippage' and time expiry.

Revenue/capital balances
The present government's policy is to increase the proportion of Urban Programme money going on capital expenditure. This particularly affects the Inner Cities Programme. Capital expenditure includes buying buildings and equipment, and short-term consultancy fees.

Many voluntary and community groups also need revenue funding, for wages and running costs. Bids must be broken down into capital and revenue elements, and it is important to realise that it may be harder to get the latter.

Slippage
Many large capital projects run behind schedule. Because ICP authorities have a set allocation for each year, they often have to look for extra capital schemes each autumn to make up their annual total. Voluntary organisations should be ready to lobby on behalf of schemes they have already submitted which have not been selected, or for additional equipment for a project in operation, if this opportunity arises. They should be aware that 'slippage' schemes are usually approved in a rush and without extensive assessment procedures. Also the money has to be spent before the end of the financial year.

Time expired projects
Urban Programme projects are usually funded for four or five years. After that, no one can agree what to do with those (the

majority) which are still meeting a need. They have become known as Time Expired Projects (TEPs).

The ideal solution is for voluntary sector TEPs to be taken onto local authority mainstream funding. The next best is continued funding through the Urban Programme. What actually happens depends on negotiations between DoE, the local authority and the projects themselves.

Further help
In most areas CVS are the first place to approach. NCVO Urban Unit supports voluntary groups using the Urban Programme. The ICP authorities usually have an inner area co-ordinator in the chief executive's department. The regional office of the Department of the Environment may also be able to help.

Other sources of funding
Urban Programme money can be combined with other sources of funding, in particular from the Manpower Services Commission. However, there is a danger in some places that staff funded by MSC will replace Urban Programme revenue funding altogether. The Urban Programme has made it possible to test new ideas because it provided continuous funding. This development puts that strength at risk because staff are funded for one year only through MSC schemes.

Other sources of statutory funding for projects run by groups in urban areas include the DHSS (Opportunities for Volunteering and the £ for £ scheme for projects for mentally handicapped people), the Commission for Racial Equality (self help fund), Department of Energy (energy saving schemes), DoE (housing association grant and derelict land grant) and joint finance, for community care projects (via the local health authority and social services department). See *Government grants: a guide for voluntary organisations* Bedford Square Press/NCVO 1983.